Crochet a Farm

19 Cute-as-Can-Be Barnyard Creations

Megan Kreiner of MK Crochet

Martingale®
Create with Confidence

Dedication

To my patient and loving husband, Michael, who puts up with a bumper crop of yarn skeins in our home, season after season.

Crochet a Farm: 19 Cute-as-Can-Be Barnyard Creations
© 2015 by Megan Kreiner

Martingale®
19021 120th Ave. NE, Ste. 102
Bothell, WA 98011-9511 USA
ShopMartingale.com

Printed in China
20 19 18 17 16 15   8 7 6 5 4 3 2 1

Library of Congress Cataloging-in-Publication Data is available upon request.

ISBN: 978-1-60468-616-6

Mission Statement

Dedicated to providing quality products and service to inspire creativity.

Credits

PUBLISHER AND CHIEF VISIONARY OFFICER
Jennifer Erbe Keltner

EDITORIAL DIRECTOR
Karen Costello Soltys

DESIGN DIRECTOR
Paula Schlosser

MANAGING EDITOR
Tina Cook

PHOTOGRAPHER
Brent Kane

ACQUISITIONS EDITOR
Karen M. Burns

PRODUCTION MANAGER
Regina Girard

TECHNICAL EDITOR
Ursula Reikes

COVER AND INTERIOR DESIGNER
Connor Chin

COPY EDITOR
Tiffany Mottet

ILLUSTRATOR
Megan Kreiner

Contents

There's More Online! For a free pattern to crochet a farmer, go to ShopMartingale.com/extras.

Introduction

Old McDonald had a farm, E-I-E-I-O. And on this farm she spun some yarn, E-I-E-I-O. With an angora rabbit here, and a woolly sheep there . . .

You get the idea. McDonald was one very happy farmer!

This book is the third in a cute-crocheted-creations series, which also includes *Crochet a Zoo* and *Bathtime Buddies.* With this book, you can create all your favorite animals from the farm, from a few simple roly-poly chickens to a whole herd of cows. For an added layer of fun, you can make wool sheep, angora bunnies, and alpaca alpacas.

I hope the lucky recipients of your farm toys enjoy the care and effort you've put into creating these adorable little animals. Happy farming and happy crocheting!

~Megan Kreiner of MK Crochet

Chickens

Don't worry about these chickens waking you up at the crack of dawn—these roly-poly little birds love to sleep in. Just don't expect them to deliver a delicious egg breakfast any time soon. You can find instructions to make eggs on page 60.

HEN

Skill Level: ■■□□

Finished Size: Approx 2½" tall and 2" long

Materials

Yarns: All yarns are DK weight 〔3〕

MC Approx 25 yds in white or brown

CC1 Approx 5 yds in yellow

CC2 Approx 5 yds in red

Approx 1 yd in black

Notions:

Size E-4 (3.5 mm) crochet hook

6 mm black plastic eyes with safety backings

Small piece of black craft felt (if not using plastic eyes)

Sewing needle and black thread for sewing felt eyes

Tapestry needle

Stuffing

Stitch markers to indicate beginning of rounds (optional)

Body

Using MC, make an 8-st adjustable ring (page 68).

Rnd 1: Sc 2 in each st around. (16 sts)

Rnd 2: *Sc 3, sc 2 in next st; rep from * 3 more times. (20 sts)

Rnd 3: *Sc 1, sc 2 in next st; rep from * 9 more times. (30 sts)

Rnds 4–8: Sc 30.

Rnd 9: *Sc 1, sc2tog; rep from * 9 more times. (20 sts)

Rnd 10: Sc 20.

Rnd 11: *Sc 3, sc2tog; rep from * 3 more times. (16 sts)

Rnds 12–14: Sc 16.

Stuff body.

Rnd 15: Sc2tog 8 times. (8 sts)

Fasten off, leaving a long tail. Close up hole unless using plastic eyes.

Wings

Make 2.

Using MC, loosely ch 6.

Rnd 1: Starting in second ch from hook and working in back ridge loops, sc 2, hdc 2, dc 5 in back ridge loop of next ch. Rotate ch so front loops are facing up. Starting in next ch and working in front loops of ch, hdc 2, sc 2. (13 sts)

Rnd 2: Sl st 2, sc 9, sl st 2.

Fasten off in first st of rnd 1 and weave in end.

Feet

Make 2.

Using CC1, loosely ch 7.

Starting in second ch from hook and working in back ridge loops, sl st 3, *ch 4, starting in second ch from hook and working in back ridge loops, sl st 3; rep from * 1 more time, cont working in back ridge loops of original ch 7, sl st 3.

Fasten off, leaving a long tail.

Comb

Using CC2, loosely ch 4.

Starting in second ch from hook and working in back ridge loops, sl st 1, ch 3, sl st in base of ch 3, sl st 1, ch 4, sl st in base of ch 4, sl st 1, ch 3, sl st in base of ch 3.

Fasten off, leaving a long tail.

Waddle

Using CC2, loosely ch 4.

Sl st in fourth ch from hook and fasten off, leaving a long tail.

Tail Feathers

Using MC, make a 7-st adjustable ring.

*Sl st 1, ch 5 to 8 sts, sl st in base of ch; rep from * 6 more times to create 7 feathers of varying lengths.

Fasten off, leaving a long tail.

Assembly

❶ Install plastic eyes between rnds 13 and 14 of body, with 3 or 4 sts between eyes. Close hole at top of head. If you prefer, sew or glue black felt circles (patt on page 75) for eyes, or use black to make French knots (page 71). Using black, sew 2 short sts above each eye for eyebrows.

Using CC1, make 6 or 7 satin sts (page 71) between eyes for a beak. Sew waddle under bottom of beak and sew comb to top and back of head.

❷ Pinch bottom half of back of body with your fingers and secure shaping with 3 or 4 running sts to make a tail shape. Sew tail feathers to middle of tail shaping.

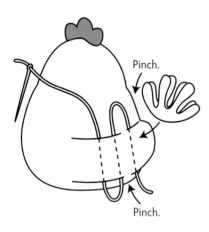

Pinch.

Pinch.

❸ With RS facing out, sew round ends of wings to shoulders. Sew feet to bottom of body.

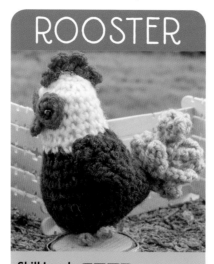

ROOSTER

Skill Level: ◼◼◻◻

Finished Size: Approx 3" tall and 2" long

Materials

Yarns: All yarns are DK weight ③

MC	Approx 20 yds in brown
A	Approx 10 yds in white
B	Approx 5 yds in yellow
C	Approx 5 yds in red
D	Approx 5 yds in blue or green

Notions:

Size E-4 (3.5 mm) crochet hook

6 mm black plastic eyes with safety backings *OR* small piece of black craft felt (if not using plastic eyes)

Sewing needle and black thread for sewing felt eyes

Tapestry needle

Stuffing

Stitch markers to indicate beginning of rounds (optional)

Eyespots

Make 2.

Using C, make an 8-st adjustable ring (page 68).

Sl st in first st of adjustable ring and gently pull partially closed (do not close hole at center of adjustable ring completely). Cut yarn, leaving a long tail.

Body

Using MC, make an 8-st adjustable ring.

Rnd 1: Sc 2 in each st around. (16 sts)

Rnd 2: *Sc 3, sc 2 in next st; rep from * 3 more times. (20 sts)

Rnd 3: *Sc 1, sc 2 in next st; rep from * 9 more times. (30 sts)

Rnds 4–8: Sc 30.

Rnd 9: *Sc 1, sc2tog; rep from * 9 more times. (20 sts)

Rnd 10: Sc 20.

Change to A.

Rnd 11: *Sc 3, sc2tog; rep from * 3 more times. (16 sts)

Rnds 12–16: Sc 16.

Stuff body.

Rnd 17: Sc2tog 8 times. (8 sts)

Fasten off, leaving a long tail. Close up hole unless using plastic eyes.

Wings

Make 2.

Using MC, loosely ch 6.

Rnd 1: Starting in second ch from hook and working in back ridge loops, sc 2, hdc 2, dc 5 in back ridge loop of next ch. Rotate ch so front loops are facing up. Starting in next ch and working in front loops of ch, hdc 2, sc 2. (13 sts)

Rnd 2: Sl st 2, sc 9, sl st 2. (13 sts)

Fasten off in first st of rnd 1 and weave in end.

Feet

Make 2.

Using B, loosely ch 7.

Starting in second ch from hook and working in back ridge loops, sl st 3, *ch 4, starting in second ch from hook and working in back ridge loops, sl st 3; rep from * 1 more time, cont working in back ridge loops of original ch 7, sl st 3.

Fasten off, leaving a long tail.

Comb

Using C, loosely ch 5.

Starting in second ch from hook and working in back ridge loops, sl st 1, ch 3, sl st in base of ch 3, *sl st 1, ch 4, sl st in base of ch 4; rep from * 1 more time, sl st 1, ch 3, sl st in base of ch 3.

Fasten off, leaving a long tail.

Double Waddle

Using C, loosely ch 4.

Sl st in fourth ch from hook, ch 4, sl st in fourth ch from hook.

Fasten off, leaving a long tail.

Small Tail Feathers

Using D, make a 7-st adjustable ring.

*Sl st 1, ch 8 to 10 sts, sl st in base st of ch; rep from * 6 more times to create 7 feathers of varying lengths.

Fasten off, leaving a long tail.

Long Tail Feathers

Using D, make a 7-st adjustable ring.

*Sl st 1, ch 12 to 15 sts, sl st in base st of ch; rep from * 6 more times to create 7 feathers of varying lengths.

Fasten off, leaving a long tail.

Assembly

❶ Slip an eyespot over post of a plastic eye, tighten eyespot ring, and then install plastic eyes between rnds 14 and 15 with 3 or 4 sts between eyes. Use leftover yarn tails to sew edges of eyespots in place. Close hole at top of head. If not using plastic eyes, sew eyespots in place, and then sew or glue black felt circles (patt on page 75) for eyes, or use black to make French knots (page 71). Using B, make 6 or 7 satin sts (page 71) between eyespots for a beak. Sew double

waddle under bottom of beak, and sew comb to top of head.

❷ Pinch bottom half of back of body with your fingers and secure shaping with 3 or 4 running sts to make a tail shape. Stack long tail feathers on top of short tail feathers and sew both sets of tail feathers to middle of tail shaping.

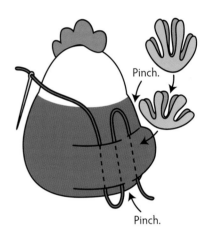

Pinch.

Pinch.

❸ With RS facing out, sew round end of wings to shoulders. Sew feet to bottom of body.

CHICK

Skill Level: ◧■◻◻

Finished Size: Approx 1½" tall and 1¼" long

Materials

Yarns: All yarns are DK weight ⓷

MC Approx 15 yds in yellow

CC Approx 2 yds in dark yellow or orange

Notions:

Size E-4 (3.5 mm) crochet hook

4 mm or 5 mm black plastic eyes with safety backings *OR* small piece of black craft felt and 1 yd black yarn (if not using plastic eyes)

Sewing needle and black thread for sewing felt eyes

Tapestry needle

Stuffing

Stitch markers to indicate beginning of rounds (optional)

Body

Using MC, make a 6-st adjustable ring (page 68).

Rnd 1: Sc 3, sc 2 in next st, sc 3 in next st, sc 2 in next st. (10 sts)

Rnd 2: Sc 3, sc 2 in each of next 7 sts. (17 sts)

Rnd 3: In bl, sc 17.

Rnds 4 and 5: Sc 17.

Rnd 6: Sc2tog, *sc 1, sc2tog; rep from * 4 more times. (11 sts)

Rnd 7: Sc 1, *sc 3, sc2tog; rep from * 1 more time. (9 sts)

Rnds 8–10: Sc 9.

Stuff body. Fasten off, leaving a long tail. Close up hole unless using plastic eyes.

Wings

Make 2.

Using MC, make an 8-st adjustable ring. *DO NOT* join last st to first st.

Fasten off, leaving a long tail.

Assembly

❶ Install plastic eyes between rnds 8 and 9, with 1 or 2 sts between eyes. Close hole at top of head. If you prefer, sew or glue black felt circles (patt on page 75) for eyes, or use black yarn to make French knots (page 71). Using CC, make 4 or 5 satin sts (page 71) between eyes for a beak. Sew wings to sides of body.

❷ Using fringe technique (page 73) and MC, cut 4 pieces, 3" long. Attach 1 piece to top of head and rem 3 pieces in a tight cluster to lower back of body. Use tapestry needle to separate yarn strands and scissors to trim and shape the fuzz.

Trim.

Ducks

You won't find an ugly duckling among the creatures in this little set! These chubby ducks love nothing more than to waddle about the farm looking for the perfect pond to paddle around in.

DUCK

Skill Level: ◨■□□

Finished Size: Approx 4" tall and 2½" long

Materials

Yarns: All yarns are DK weight ③

MC   Approx 25 yds in white

CC   Approx 5 yds in yellow

Approx 1 yd in black

Notions:

Size E-4 (3.5 mm) crochet hook

6 mm black plastic eyes with safety backings *OR* small piece of black craft felt (if not using plastic eyes)

Sewing needle and black thread for sewing felt eyes

Tapestry needle

Stuffing

Stitch markers to indicate beginning of rounds (optional)

Body

Using MC, make an 8-st adjustable ring (page 68).

Rnd 1: Sc 2 in each st around. (16 sts)

Rnd 2: *Sc 3, sc 2 in next st; rep from * 3 more times. (20 sts)

Rnd 3: *Sc 1, sc 2 in next st; rep from * 9 more times. (30 sts)

Rnds 4–8: Sc 30.

Rnd 9: *Sc 1, sc2tog; rep from * 9 more times. (20 sts)

Rnd 10: Sc 20.

Rnd 11: *Sc 3, sc2tog; rep from * 3 more times. (16 sts)

Rnds 12–14: Sc 16.

Rnd 15: *Sc 2, sc2tog; rep from * 3 more times. (12 sts)

Rnds 16–19: Sc 12.

Rnd 20: Sc 2 in each st around. (24 sts)

Rnd 21: *Sc 6, sc2tog; rep from * 2 more times. (21 sts)

Rnds 22 and 23: Sc 21.

Rnd 24: *Sc 1, sc2tog; rep from * 6 more times. (14 sts)

Rnd 25: Sc 14.

Stuff body, neck and head.

Rnd 26: Sc2tog 7 times. (7 sts)

Stuff body. Fasten off, leaving a long tail. Close up hole unless using plastic eyes.

Wings

Make 2.

Using MC, loosely ch 6.

Rnd 1: Starting in second ch from hook and working in back ridge loops, sc 2, hdc 2, dc 5 in back ridge loop of next ch. Rotate ch so front loops are facing up. Starting in next ch and working in front loops of ch, hdc 2, sc 2. (13 sts)

Rnd 2: Sl st 2, sc 9, sl st 2.

Fasten off in first st of rnd 1 and weave in end.

Feet

Make 2.

Using CC, make a 7-st adjustable ring. *DO NOT* join.

Ch 1, turn.

Sk first ch, sl st 3, *ch 3, sl st in base of ch 3, sl st 1; rep from * 2 more times, sl st 1.

Fasten off in first ch 1, leaving a long tail.

Tail Feathers

Using MC, make a 4-st adjustable ring.

*Sl st 1, ch 5 to 7 sts, sl st in base of ch; rep from * 3 more times to create 4 feathers of varying lengths.

Fasten off, leaving a long tail.

Beak

Using CC, loosely ch 6.

Rnd 1: Starting in second ch from hook and working in back ridge loops, sc 4, sc 3 in back ridge loop of next ch. Rotate ch so front loops are facing up. Starting in next ch and working in front loops of ch, sc 3, sc 2 in next st. (12 sts)

Rnds 2 and 3: Sc 12.

Fasten off. Flatten seam and sew closed, leaving a long tail.

Assembly

1 Install plastic eyes between rnds 13 and 14, with 3 or 4 sts between eyes. Close hole at top of head. If you prefer, sew or glue black felt circles (patt on page 75) for eyes, or use black to make French knots (page 71). Using black, sew 2 short sts above each eye for eyebrows. Sew sewn edge of beak to front of head below eyes.

2 Using MC, attach yarn to back of neck at base of head. Make a running stitch down back of neck to shoulders, pulling yarn firmly, to add curve to neck. Fasten off and weave in end.

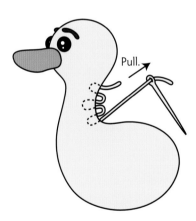

3 Pinch bottom half of back of body with your fingers and secure shaping with 3 or 4 running sts to make a tail shape. Sew tail feathers to middle of tail shaping.

Pinch.

Pinch.

4 With RS facing out, sew round ends of wings to shoulders. Sew feet to bottom of body.

DUCKLING

Skill Level: ◼◻◻

Finished Size: Approx 1½" tall and 1¼" long

Materials

Yarn: All yarns are DK weight 🧶3

MC Approx 10 yds in white

CC Approx 5 yds in dark yellow or orange

Notions:

Size E-4 (3.5 mm) crochet hook

4 mm or 5 mm black plastic eyes with safety backings *OR* small piece of black craft felt (if not using plastic eyes)

Sewing needle and black thread for sewing felt eyes

Tapestry needle

Stuffing

Stitch markers to indicate beginning of rounds (optional)

Body

Using MC, make a 6-st adjustable ring (page 68).

Rnd 1: Sc 3, sc 2 in next st, sc 3 in next st, sc 2 in next st. (10 sts)

Rnd 2: Sc 3, sc 2 in each of next 7 sts. (17 sts)

Rnd 3: In bl, sc 17.

Rnds 4 and 5: Sc 17.

Rnd 6: Sc2tog, *sc 1, sc2tog; rep from * 4 more times. (11 sts)

Rnd 7: Sc 1, *sc 3, sc2tog; rep from * 1 more time. (9 sts)

Rnds 8–10: Sc 9.

Stuff body. Fasten off, leaving a long tail. Close up hole unless using plastic eyes.

Wings

Make 2.

Using MC, make an 8-st adjustable ring. *DO NOT* join last st to first st.

Fasten off, leaving a long tail for sewing.

Beak

Using CC, loosely ch 5.

Starting in second ch from hook and working in back ridge loops, sc 4.

Fasten off, leaving a long tail.

Assembly

❶ Install plastic eyes between rnds 8 and 9, with 1 or 2 sts between eyes. Close hole at top of head. If you prefer, sew or glue black felt circles (patt on page 75) for eyes, or use black to make French knots (page 71). Sew flat edge of beak to front of head directly below eyes. Sew wings to sides of body.

❷ Pinch bottom half of back of body with your fingers and secure shaping with 2 or 3 running sts to make a tail shape.

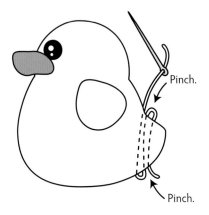

❸ Cut 4 pieces of white, 3" long. Using fringe technique (page 73), attach 1 piece of yarn to top of head and rem 3 pieces in a tight cluster to middle of tail shape. Use tapestry needle to separate yarn strands and scissors to trim and shape the fuzz.

Rabbit

These adorable little bunnies are sweet and snuggly, and they'd never dream of raiding Farmer McDonald's kitchen garden. You can easily adjust the ears to be floppy or upright. It would seem a shame not to make more than one. Look for instructions to make a carrot on page 59.

Skill Level: ◖■□□ **Finished Size:** Approx 3" tall and 3½" long

Materials

Yarns: All yarns are DK weight (3)

MC   Approx 50 yds for bunny
CC1 Approx 10 yds white
CC2 Approx 5 yds black

Notions:

Size E-4 (3.5 mm) crochet hook

6 mm black plastic eyes with safety backings

Small scrap of beige or light-pink craft felt for inner ears

Small piece of black craft felt (if not using plastic eyes)

Sewing needle and thread to match felt for sewing felt ears and eyes

Tapestry needle

Stuffing

Stitch markers to indicate beginning of rounds (optional)

Note: Use MC throughout, except where noted.

Head and Body

Make an 8-st adjustable ring (page 68).

Rnd 1: Sc 2 in each st around. (16 sts)

Rnd 2: *Sc 3, sc 2 in next st; rep from * 3 more times. (20 sts)

Rnd 3: *Sc 1, sc 2 in next st; rep from * 9 more times. (30 sts)

Rnd 4: Sc 30.

Rnd 5: *Sc 1, sc2tog; rep from * 9 more times. (20 sts)

Rnd 6: *Sc 3, sc2tog; rep from * 3 more times. (16 sts)

Rnd 7: Sc2tog 8 times. (8 sts)
Lightly stuff head. If using plastic eyes, install them at center of head with 2 sts between eyes. Finish stuffing head.

Rnd 8: Sc 2 in each st around. (16 sts)

Rnd 9: Sc 16.

Rnd 10: *Sc 7, sc 2 in next st; rep from * 1 more time. (18 sts)

Rnd 11: Sc 18.

Rnd 12: *Sc 5, sc 2 in next st; rep from * 2 more times. (21 sts)

Rnd 13: Sc 21.

Rnd 14: *Sc 6, sc 2 in next st; rep from * 2 more times. (24 sts)

Rnd 15: Sc2tog 12 times. (12 sts)
Stuff body.

Rnd 16: Sc2tog 6 times. (6 sts)
Fasten off, close up hole, and weave in end.

Front Paws

Make 2.
Make a 4-st adjustable ring.

Rnd 1: Sc 2 in each st around. (8 sts)

Rnd 2: Sc 8.

Rnd 3: *Sc 2, sc2tog; rep from * 1 more time. (6 sts)

Rnd 4: Sc 6.

Stuff paw and fasten off, leaving a long tail.

Back Paws

Make 2.

Make a 5-st adjustable ring.

Rnd 1: Sc 2 in each st around. (10 sts)

Rnds 2 and 3: Sc 10.

Rnd 4: *Sc 3, sc2tog; rep from * 1 more time. (8 sts)

Rnds 5 and 6: Sc 8.

Stuff paw.

Rnd 7: *Sc 2, sc2tog; rep from * 1 more time. (6 sts)

Fasten off, close up hole, and weave in end.

Back Legs

Make 2.

Make an 8-st adjustable ring.

Rnd 1: Sc 2 in each st around. (16 sts)

Rnd 2: *Sc 2, sc2tog; rep from * 3 more times. (12 sts)

Stuff leg and fasten off, leaving a long tail.

Ears

Make 2.

Loosely ch 8.

Rnd 1: Starting in second ch from hook and working in back ridge loops, sc 3, hdc 3, sc 4 in back ridge loop of next ch. Rotate ch so front loops are facing up. Starting in next ch and working in front loops of ch, hdc 3, sc 2, (sc 1, hdc 1) in next ch. (17 sts)

Rnd 2: Sl st 16, sc 3 in next st. (19 sts)

Fasten off, leaving a long tail.

Assembly

❶ Using MC and a tapestry needle, insert needle under chin and draw out through center of face. Rep 2 or 3 times and pull tightly to create cheeks. Using CC2, embroider a Y shape to front of face for lip cleft and nose. If not using plastic eyes, sew or glue black felt circles (patt on page 75) for eyes, or use CC2 to make French knots (page 71) directly above nose. Using CC2, sew 2 short sts above each eye for eyebrows.

❷ Sew open edges of legs to back lower half of body at hips and stuff before closing seam. With larger ends of paws facing forward, sew paws to bottom of legs and body. Position closed seams of front paws at shoulders and whipstitch in place.

❸ Cut out 2 ear patches (patt on page 75) from light pink or beige felt. Sew or glue patches to RS of ears and attach ears to either top of head (for stand-up ears), or to sides of head (for floppy ears).

Stand-up ears

Floppy ears

❹ Cut 6" length of CC1. Then wrap remaining CC1 around 3 fingers 20 times and cut top and bottom of loops. Tie 6" piece of yarn tightly around middle of cut strands. Trim to create a pom-pom; attach it to back of rabbit.

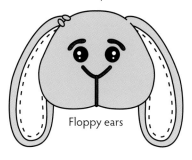

Pigs

These little piggies are more than happy to stay at home and relax in the sunshine. Make a whole litter of piglets so they'll have company while playing together in their favorite mud puddle.

PIG

Skill Level: ■■□□

Finished Size: Approx 4" tall and 5" long

Materials

Yarns: All yarns are worsted weight (4)

MC Approx 120 yds in pink

Approx 1 yd in black

Notions:

Size G-6 (4 mm) crochet hook

9 mm black plastic eyes with safety backings

Small piece of black craft felt (if not using plastic eyes)

Sewing needle and black thread for sewing felt eyes

Tapestry needle

Stuffing

Stitch markers to indicate beginning of rounds (optional)

Note: Use MC throughout, except where noted.

Head

Loosely ch 7.

Rnd 1: Starting in second ch from hook and working in back ridge loops, sc 5, sc 8 in back ridge loop of next ch. Rotate ch so front loops are facing up. Starting in next ch and working in front loops of ch, sc 4, sc 7 in next ch. (24 sts)

Rnd 2: Sc 2 in next st, sc 4, sc 2 in each of next 8 sts, sc 4, sc 2 in each of next 7 sts. (40 sts)

Rnd 3: Sc 14, hdc 7, sc 6, hdc 7, sc 6. (40 sts)

Rnds 4-6: Sc 40.

Rnd 7: *Sc 3, sc2tog; rep from * 7 more times. (32 sts)

Rnd 8: *Sc 2, sc2tog; rep from * 7 more times. (24 sts)

Rnd 9: *Sc 1, sc2tog; rep from * 7 more times. (16 sts)

Rnd 10: *Sc 2, sc2tog; rep from * 3 more times. (12 sts)

Stuff head.

Rnd 11: *Sc 1, sc2tog; rep from * 3 more times. (8 sts)

Fasten off, leaving a long tail. Close up hole unless using plastic eyes.

Body

Make an 8-st adjustable ring (page 68).

Rnd 1: Sc 2 in each st around. (16 sts)

Rnd 2: *Sc 3, sc 2 in next st; rep from * 3 more times. (20 sts)

Rnd 3: *Sc 1, sc 2 in next st; rep from * 9 more times. (30 sts)

Rnds 4-8: Sc 30.

Rnd 9: *Sc 1, sc2tog; rep from * 9 more times. (20 sts)

Rnd 10: Sc 20.

Rnd 11: *Sc 3, sc2tog; rep from * 3 more times. (16 sts)

Rnd 12: Sc 16.

Rnd 13: Sc2tog 8 times. (8 sts)

Stuff body.

Rnd 14: *Sc 2, sc2tog; rep from * 1 more time. (6 sts)

Fasten off, leaving a long tail. Close up hole and weave in end.

Legs

Make 4.

Make a 6-st adjustable ring.

Rnd 1: Sc 3, sc 2 in next st, sc 3 in next st, sc 2 in next st. (10 sts)

Rnd 2: Sc 3, sc 2 in each of next 7 sts. (17 sts)

Rnd 3: In bl, sc 17.

Rnd 4: Sc 17.

Rnd 5: Sc 1, sc2tog 8 times. (9 sts)

Rnds 6-8: Sc 9.

Stuff leg.

Rnd 9: *Sc 1, sc2tog; rep from * 2 more times. (6 sts)

Fasten off, leaving a long tail. Close up hole and weave in end.

Tail

Loosely ch 12. Starting in second ch from hook and working in back ridge loops, sc 2 in each of next 11 chs and fasten off, leaving a long tail.

Nose

Make a 6-st adjustable ring.

Rnd 1: Sc 2 in each st around. (12 sts)

Rnd 2: Sc 12.

Rnd 3: Sc2tog 6 times. (6 sts) Stuff and fasten off, leaving a long tail.

Ears

Make 2.

Loosely ch 6.

Starting in second ch from hook and working in back ridge loops, sc 2, hdc 2, dc 5 in back ridge loop of next ch. Rotate ch so front loops are facing up. Starting in next ch and working in front loops of ch, hdc 2, sc 2. Sl st at top of ch and fasten off, leaving a long tail.

Assembly

❶ Sew open edge of stuffed nose to front of head. Install plastic eyes directly above nose, with 2 or 3 sts between eyes. Close hole at top of head. If you prefer, sew or glue black felt circles (patt on page 75) for eyes, or use black to make French knots (page 71). Using black, embroider eyebrows above eyes using lazy daisy st (page 71), and sew 2 short sts to front of nose for nostrils. Sew ears to top of head above eyebrows. Fold ear over and secure in place using leftover yarn tail at top of ear.

Fold.

❷ With larger end of body in back, attach head to top front of body. Attach legs halfway up sides of body. Attach tail to back of body.

❸ To keep legs from splaying out, attach yarn to inside surface of one leg, pass yarn through body to inside surface of opposite leg, then back again through body to starting point. Pull gently to draw legs close to body. To form hooves, use pink yarn and a tapestry needle and draw a long st of yarn from middle of foot in front to middle of foot in back 2 or 3 times, pulling tightly as you sew. Rep on other 3 feet.

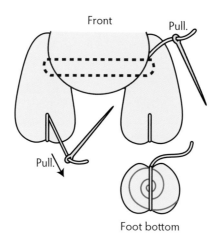

Front

Pull.

Pull.

Foot bottom

PIGLET

Skill Level: ◧■◻◻

Finished Size: Approx 2¼" tall and 3½" long

Materials

Yarns: All yarns are DK weight 🧶**3**

Approx 25 yds in pink

Approx 1 yd in black

Notions:

Size D-3 (3.25 mm) crochet hook

6 mm black plastic eyes with safety backings

Small piece of black craft felt (if not using plastic eyes)

Sewing needle and black thread for sewing felt eyes

Tapestry needle

Stuffing

Stitch markers to indicate beginning of rounds (optional)

Note: Use pink throughout, except where noted.

Head and Body

Make an 8-st adjustable ring (page 68).

Rnd 1: Sc 2 in each st around. (16 sts)

Rnd 2: *Sc 3, sc 2 in next st; rep from * 3 more times. (20 sts)

Rnd 3: *Sc 1, sc 2 in next st; rep from * 9 more times. (30 sts)

Rnd 4: Sc 30.

Rnd 5: *Sc 1, sc2tog; rep from * 9 more times. (20 sts)

Rnd 6: *Sc 3, sc2tog; rep from * 3 more times. (16 sts)

Rnd 7: Sc2tog 8 times. (8 sts)

Lightly stuff head. If using plastic safety eyes, install them between rnds 1 and 2, with 2 or 3 sts between eyes. Finish stuffing head.

Rnd 8: Sc 2 in each st around. (16 sts)

Rnd 9: Sc 16.

Rnd 10: *Sc 7, sc 2 in next st; rep from * 1 more time. (18 sts)

Rnd 11: Sc 18.

Rnd 12: *Sc 5, sc 2 in next st; rep from * 2 more times. (21 sts)

Rnd 13: Sc 21.

Rnd 14: *Sc 6, sc 2 in next st; rep from * 2 more times. (24 sts)

Rnd 15: Sc2tog 12 times. (12 sts) Stuff body.

Rnd 16: Sc2tog 6 times. (6 sts)

Make tail: Ch 7, sk first ch, sc 2 in next 6 chs.

Fasten off. Close up hole and weave in end.

Nose and Legs

Make 5.

Make a 6-st adjustable ring.

Rnd 1: Sc 2 in each st around. (12 sts)

Rnd 2: Sc 12.

Rnd 3: Sc2tog 6 times. (6 sts)

Stuff and fasten off, leaving a long tail.

Ears

Make 2.

Loosely ch 6.

Starting in second ch from hook and working in back ridge loops, sc 2, hdc 2, dc 5 in back ridge loop of next ch. Rotate ch so front loops are facing up. Starting in next ch and working in front loops of ch, hdc 2, sc 2.

Sl st at top of ch and fasten off, leaving a long tail.

Assembly

❶ Sew open end of stuffed nose to front of head. If not using plastic safety eyes, sew or glue on black felt circles (patt on page 75) for eyes, or use black to make French knots (page 71)

directly above nose. Using black, sew 2 short sts above each eye for eyebrows, and 2 pairs of short sts to front of nose for nostrils. Sew ears to top of head above eyebrows. Fold ear over and secure in place using leftover yarn tail at top of ear.

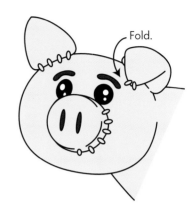

❷ Using pink and a tapestry needle, insert needle under chin and out directly under nose. Rep 2 or 3 times and pull tightly to create cheeks.

❸ Sew open edges of stuffed legs to bottom of body.

Cow

Make a whole herd of cows by switching up just a few of the details. Change the yarn colors and crochet your favorite breeds using white yarn with black spots for a Holstein, brown yarn for a Jersey, or black yarn for a Black Angus. There are even instructions for making a milk pail on page 58!

Skill Level: ◖■▢▭   **Finished Size:** Approx 5" tall and 7" long

Materials

Yarns: All yarns are worsted weight (4)

MC   Approx 150 yds in white

CC1   Approx 30 yds in pink or beige

CC2   Approx 20 yds in yellow

Approx 5 yds in black

Notions:

Size G-6 (4 mm) crochet hook

9 mm black plastic eyes with safety backings *OR* small piece of black craft felt (if not using plastic eyes)

Small piece of black or brown craft felt (optional for spots)

Sewing needle and thread to match felt for sewing felt spots and eyes

Tapestry needle

Stuffing

Stitch markers to indicate beginning of rounds (optional)

Head

Using CC1, loosely ch 7.

Rnd 1: Starting in second ch from hook and working in back ridge loops, sc 5, sc 5 in back ridge loop of next ch. Rotate ch so front loops are facing up. Starting in next ch and working in front loops of ch, sc 4, sc 4 in next ch. (18 sts)

Making a Calf or Bull

To make a calf, use DK-weight yarn, a size D-3 (3.25 mm) crochet hook, and 9 mm plastic eyes with safety backings, and omit the teats. Calf will be approx 3½" tall and 4" long.

To make a bull, work as for cow in desired colors and use "Long Bull Horns" on page 24. If you want to make a really big bull, use bulky-weight yarn, a size I-9 (5.5 mm) crochet hook, and 12 mm eyes.

Rnd 2: Sc 2 in next st, sc 4, sc 2 in each of next 5 sts, sc 4, sc 2 in each of next 4 sts. (28 sts)

Rnd 3: Sc 9, sc 2 in each of next 4 sts, sc 10, sc 2 in each of next 4 sts, sc 1. (36 sts)

Rnds 4–6: Sc 36.

Rnd 7: *Sc 2, sc2tog; rep from * 8 more times. (27 sts)

Rnd 8: *Sc 1, sc2tog; rep from * 8 more times. (18 sts)

Change to MC.

Rnd 9: Sc2tog 9 times. (9 sts)

Rnd 10: *Hdc 1, hdc 3 in next st, hdc 1; rep from * 2 more times. (15 sts)

Rnd 11: Hdc 1, *hdc 2 in next st, hdc 1; rep from * 6 more times. (22 sts)

Rnds 12 and 13: Sc 22.

Rnd 14: Sc 1, *sc2tog, sc 1; rep from * 6 more times. (15 sts)

Rnd 15: *Sc 1, sc2tog; rep from * 4 more times. (10 sts)

Stuff head.

Rnd 16: *Sc 3, sc2tog; rep from * 1 more time. (8 sts)

Fasten off, leaving a long tail. Close up hole unless using plastic eyes.

Body

Using MC, make an 8-st adjustable ring (page 68).

Rnd 1: Sc 2 in each st around. (16 sts)

Rnd 2: *Sc 3, sc 2 in next st; rep from * 3 more times. (20 sts)

Rnd 3: *Sc 1, sc 2 in next st; rep from * 9 more times. (30 sts)

Rnds 4–8: Sc 30.

Rnd 9: *Sc 1, sc2tog; rep from * 9 more times. (20 sts)

Rnd 10: Sc 20.

Rnd 11: *Sc 3, sc2tog; rep from * 3 more times. (16 sts)

Rnd 12: Sc 16.

Rnd 13: Sc2tog 8 times. (8 sts)

Stuff body.

Rnd 14: *Sc 2, sc2tog; rep from * 1 more time. (6 sts)

Fasten off, leaving a long tail.

Fasten off with a sl st in next st and weave in end.

Nostrils

Make 2.

Using CC1 to match muzzle, loosely ch 7.

Starting in second ch from hook, sc in next 6 sc.

Fasten off, leaving a long tail.

Udder

Skip if making calf.

Using CC1, make a 6-st adjustable ring.

Rnd 1: Sc 2 in each st around. (12 sts)

Rnds 2 and 3: Sc 12.

Fasten off, leaving a long tail.

Teats

Skip if making calf.

Make 4.

Using CC1, make a 4-st adjustable ring.

Fasten off in first st, leaving a long tail.

Long Bull Horns

Skip if making calf or cow.

Make 2.

Using CC2 or MC, make a 6-st adjustable ring.

Rnd 1: In bl, sc 6.

Rnds 2–4: Sc 6.

Legs

Make 4.

Using CC2, make a 6-st adjustable ring.

Rnd 1: Sc 3, sc 2 in next st, sc 3 in next st, sc 2 in next st. (10 sts)

Rnd 2: Sc 3, sc 2 in each of next 7 sts. (17 sts)

Rnd 3: In bl, sc 17.

Rnds 4 and 5: Sc 17.

Change to MC.

Rnd 6: In bl, sc 1, sc2tog 8 times. (9 sts)

Rnds 7–10: Sc 9.

Stuff leg.

Rnd 11: Sc 1, sc2tog 4 times. (5 sts)

Fasten off. Flatten seam and sew closed, leaving a long tail.

Tail

Using MC, make a 6-st adjustable ring.

Rnd 1: Sc 2 in each st around. (12 sts)

Rnds 2 and 3: Sc 12.

Rnd 4: Sc2tog 6 times. (6 sts)

Stuff and fasten off, leaving a long tail.

Cow Horns

Skip if making calf.

Make 2.

Using CC2, make a 5-st adjustable ring.

Sc 5.

Fasten off, leaving a long tail.

Ears

Make 2.

Using MC, loosely ch 6.

Starting in second ch from hook and working in back ridge loops, sc 2, hdc 2, dc 5 in back ridge loop of next ch. Rotate ch so front loops are facing up. Starting in next ch and working in front loops of ch, hdc 2, sc 2. (13 sts)

Rnd 5: *Sc 1, sc2tog; rep from * 1 more time. (4 sts)

Rnd 6: Sc 4.

Rnd 7: Sk 1 st, sl st 1.

Fasten off, leaving a long tail.

Assembly

❶ Install plastic eyes to front of head, with 2 or 3 sts between eyes. Close hole at back of head. If you prefer, sew or glue on black felt circles (patt on page 75) for eyes, or use black to make French knots (page 71). Embroider eyebrows above eyes with black using lazy daisy st (page 71). Fold nostrils in half and sew ends tog to form a teardrop shape. Attach nostrils to front corners of muzzle. Attach ears to sides of head 1 row above eyebrows. *For cow horns,* attach open end of horns to top of head.

For bull horns, attach open edges of horns to top sides of head. Using leftover yarn from top of horn, sew a running st (page 71) down back of horn from tip to base and pull gently to curve horn. Secure and weave in ends.

❷ Close up hole at front of body and weave in end. Attach cow head to smaller front end of body. If making bull, attach bull head to large end of body. Attach legs halfway up sides of body. Stuff and attach open edge of tail to body. Cut 8 to 10 pieces of black, 4" long. Using fringe technique (page 73), attach to tail. Use tapestry needle to separate yarn strands and scissors to trim and shape hair.

❸ For spotted cow on page 22, cut 5 to 7 spots (patt on page 75) from black felt. Pin spots in place, and then attach them with either a running st (page 71) or washable fabric glue.

❹ To add an udder to your cow, sew teats onto udder first before stuffing. Sew udder in place.

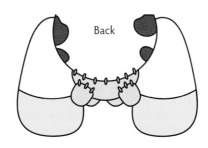

❺ To keep legs from splaying out, attach yarn to inside surface of one leg, pass yarn through body to inside surface of opposite leg, then back again

through body to starting point. Pull gently to draw legs close to body. To form hooves, use yellow yarn and a tapestry needle, loop a long stitch of yarn from top of foot in front to top of foot in back 2 or 3 times, pulling tightly as you sew. Rep on other 3 feet.

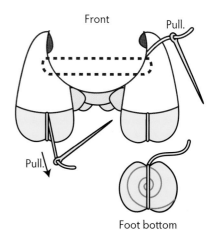

Color Variations for Cows

Want to make a Jersey cow with a brown-tipped nose or add a center stripe to your calf's face? *For a face stripe,* make an extra ear, position the shape between the eyes with the largest part pointed up, and sew it in place. *For a color-tipped nose,* start with your yarn for the nose, and then change to white yarn at round 6. Finally, change to main color yarn at round 9 per pattern instructions and continue to work to the end.

Horse

These horses are more than happy to spend their days hanging out and gossiping with the cows instead of dragging a plow around the fields. However, they love to race around the barn whenever the donkey is up for it!

Skill Level: ■■□□   **Finished Size:** Approx 6" tall and 5" long

Materials

Yarns: All yarns are worsted weight (4)

MC Approx 125 yds in light brown

CC1 Approx 25 yds in dark brown

CC2 Approx 15 yds in charcoal

Approx 1 yd in black

Notions:

Size G-6 (4 mm) crochet hook

8 mm or 9 mm black plastic eyes with safety backings

Small piece of black craft felt (if not using plastic eyes)

Sewing needle and black thread for sewing felt eyes

Tapestry needle

Stuffing

Stitch markers to indicate beginning of rounds (optional)

Note: Use MC throughout, except where noted.

Making a Foal

To make a foal, use DK-weight yarn, a size D-3 (3.25 mm) crochet hook, and 9 mm plastic eyes with safety backings. The foal will be approx 4½" tall and 4" long.

Head

Make an 8-st adjustable ring (page 68).

Rnd 1: Sc 2 in each st around. (16 sts)

Rnd 2: Sc 16.

Rnd 3: *Sc 7, sc 2 in next st; rep from * 1 more time. (18 sts)

Rnds 4–6: Sc 18.

Rnd 7: *Sc 8, sc 2 in next st; rep from * 1 more time. (20 sts)

Rnds 8 and 9: Sc 20.

Rnd 10: *Sc 4, sc 2 in next st; rep from * 3 more times. (24 sts)

Rnds 11 and 12: Sc 24.

Rnd 13: *Sc 1, sc2tog; rep from * 7 more times. (16 sts)

Rnd 14: *Sc 2, sc2tog; rep from * 3 more times. (12 sts)

Stuff head.

Rnd 15: *Sc 1, sc2tog; rep from * 3 more times. (8 sts)

Fasten off, leaving a long tail. Close up hole unless using plastic eyes.

Body

Make an 8-st adjustable ring.

Rnd 1: Sc 2 in each st around. (16 sts)

Rnd 2: *Sc 3, sc 2 in next st; rep from * 3 more times. (20 sts)

Rnd 3: *Sc 1, sc 2 in next st; rep from * 9 more times. (30 sts)

Rnds 4–8: Sc 30.

Rnd 9: *Sc 1, sc2tog; rep from * 9 more times. (20 sts)

Rnd 10: Sc 20.

Rnd 11: *Sc 3, sc2tog; rep from * 3 more times. (16 sts)

Rnd 12: Sc 16.

Rnd 13: Sc2tog 8 times. (8 sts)

Stuff body.

Rnd 14: *Sc 2, sc2tog; rep from * 1 more time. (6 sts)

Fasten off, close up hole, and weave in end.

Neck

Ch 20 and join with a sl st to form a ring, taking care not to twist sts.

Rnds 1 and 2: Sc 20.

Rnd 3: *Sc 3, sc2tog; rep from * 3 more times. (16 sts)

Rnd 4: *Sc 2, sc2tog; rep from * 3 more times. (12 sts)

Fasten off, leaving a long tail.

Nostrils

Make 2.

Loosely ch 7.

Starting in second ch from hook and working in back ridge loops, sc 6.

Fasten off, leaving a long tail.

Ears

Make 2.

Loosely ch 6.

Starting in second ch from hook and working in back ridge loops, sc 2, hdc 2, dc 5 in back ridge loop of next ch. Rotate ch so front loops are facing up. Starting in next ch and working in front loops of ch, hdc 2, sc 2. (13 sts)

Fasten off in first st of rnd 1 and weave in end.

Legs

Make 4.

Using CC2, make a 6-st adjustable ring.

Rnd 1: Sc 3, sc 2 in next st, sc 3 in next st, sc 2 in next st. (10 sts)

Rnd 2: Sc 3, sc 2 in each of next 7 sts. (17 sts)

Rnd 3: In bl, sc 17.

Rnds 4 and 5: Sc 17.

Change to MC.

Rnd 6: Sc 1, sc2tog 8 times. (9 sts)

Rnds 7–10: Sc 9.

Stuff leg.

Rnd 11: Sc 1, sc2tog 4 times. (5 sts)

Fasten off. Flatten seam and sew closed, leaving a long tail.

Assembly

① Install plastic eyes to sides of head between rnds 8 and 9 with 8 sts between eyes. Close hole at back of head. If you prefer, sew or glue on black felt circles (patt on page 75) for eyes, or use black to make French knots (page 71). Embroider eyebrows above eyes with black using lazy daisy st (page 71). Fold nostrils in half and sew ends tog to form a teardrop shape. Attach nostrils to front of muzzle with 3 sts between them. Attach ears to sides of head 2 rows above eyes.

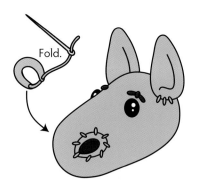

② Pin and sew larger open edge of neck to top of larger, rounder end of body. Attach head to open end of neck and stuff neck before closing seam. Attach legs halfway up sides of body.

③ Cut 35 to 40 pieces of CC1, 4" long. Using fringe technique (page 73), attach to top of head and down back of neck. Use tapestry needle to separate yarn strands and scissors to trim and shape the mane.

④ To keep legs from splaying out, attach yarn to inside surface of one leg, pass yarn through body to inside surface of opposite leg, then back again through body to starting point. Pull gently to draw legs close to

body. To form hooves, use CC2 and a tapestry needle, draw and loop a long st of yarn from top of foot in back to bottom center of foot 2 or 3 times, pulling tightly as you sew. Rep on other 3 feet.

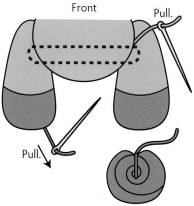

⑤ Cut 5 pieces of CC1, 8" long, and while holding all strands tog, use fringe technique to attach bundle to back of horse using a large crochet hook. Use tapestry needle to separate yarn strands and scissors to trim.

Donkey

This donkey is about as stubborn as she is cute! However, she loves nothing more than to challenge the farm horses to a race whenever she can, because, when she wants to move, she can really haul her . . . um . . . "donkey keister."

Skill Level: ■■□□ **Finished Size:** Approx 5½" tall and 5½" long

Materials

Yarns: All yarns are worsted weight (4)

MC Approx 110 yds in gray

CC1 Approx 20 yds in black

CC2 Approx 10 yds in off-white

Notions:

Size G-6 (4 mm) crochet hook

8 mm or 9 mm black plastic eyes with safety backings

Small piece of off-white craft felt for inner ear and belly

Small piece of black craft felt (if not using plastic eyes)

Sewing needle and thread to match felt for sewing felt ears and eyes

Tapestry needle

Stuffing

Stitch markers to indicate beginning of rounds (optional)

Head

Using CC2, make an 8-st adjustable ring (page 68).

Rnd 1: Sc 2 in each st around. (16 sts)

Rnd 2: *Sc 3, sc 2 in next st; rep from * 3 more times. (20 sts)

Rnds 3–5: Sc 20.

Rnd 6: *Sc 3, sc2tog; rep from * 3 more times. (16 sts)

Change to MC.

Rnd 7: Sc2tog 8 times. (8 sts)

Rnd 8: Sc 2 in each st around. (16 sts)

Rnd 9: Sc 16.

Rnd 10: *Sc 7, sc 2 in next st; rep from * 1 more time. (18 sts)

Rnd 11: Sc 18.

Rnd 12: *Sc 5, sc 2 in next st; rep from * 2 more times. (21 sts)

Rnds 13 and 14: Sc 21.

Rnd 15: *Sc 6, sc 2 in next st; rep from * 2 more times. (24 sts)

Rnd 16: Sc2tog 12 times. (12 sts)

Stuff head.

Rnd 17: *Sc 1, sc2tog; rep from * 3 more times. (8 sts)

Fasten off, leaving a long tail. Close up hole unless using plastic eyes.

Body

Using MC, make an 8-st adjustable ring.

Rnd 1: Sc 2 in each st around. (16 sts)

Rnd 2: *Sc 3, sc 2 in next st; rep from * 3 more times. (20 sts)

Rnd 3: *Sc 1, sc 2 in next st; rep from * 9 more times. (30 sts)

Rnds 4–8: Sc 30.

Rnd 9: *Sc 1, sc2tog; rep from * 9 more times. (20 sts)

Rnd 10: Sc 20.

Rnd 11: *Sc 3, sc2tog; rep from * 3 more times. (16 sts)

Rnd 12: Sc 16.

Rnd 13: Sc2tog 8 times. (8 sts)

Stuff body.

Rnd 14: Sc2tog 4 times. (4 sts)

Fasten off, close up hole, and weave in end.

Neck

Using MC, ch 20 and join with a sl st to form a ring, taking care not to twist sts.

Rnds 1 and 2: Sc 20.

Rnd 3: *Sc 3, sc2tog; rep from * 3 more times. (16 sts)

Rnd 4: *Sc 2, sc2tog; rep from * 3 more times. (12 sts)

Fasten off, leaving a long tail.

Nostrils

Make 2.

Using CC2, loosely ch 7.

Starting in second ch from hook and working in back ridge loops, sc 6.

Fasten off, leaving a long tail.

Ears

Make 2.

Using MC, loosely ch 8.

Rnd 1: Starting in second ch from hook and working in back ridge loops, sc 3, hdc 3, sc 4 in back ridge loop of next ch. Rotate work so front loops of ch are facing up. Starting in next ch and working in front loops of ch, hdc 3, sc 2, (sc 1, hdc 1) in next ch. (17 sts)

Rnd 2: Sl st 16, sc 3 in next st. (19 sts)

Fasten off, leaving a long tail.

Tail

Using MC, make a 6-st adjustable ring.

Rnd 1: Sc 2 in each st around. (12 sts)

Rnds 2 and 3: Sc 12.

Rnd 4: Sc2tog 6 times. (6 sts) Stuff and fasten off, leaving a long tail.

Legs

Make 4.

Using CC1, make a 6-st adjustable ring.

Rnd 1: Sc 3, sc 2 in next st, sc 3 in next st, sc 2 in next st. (10 sts)

Rnd 2: Sc 3, sc 2 in each of next 7 sts. (17 sts)

Rnd 3: In bl, sc 17.

Rnds 4 and 5: Sc 17.

Change to MC.

Rnd 6: Sc 1, sc2tog 8 times. (9 sts)

Rnds 7-10: Sc 9.

Stuff leg.

Rnd 11: Sc 1, sc2tog 4 times. (5 sts)

Fasten off. Flatten seam and sew closed, leaving a long tail.

Assembly

❶ Install plastic eyes to sides of head 3 rnds above color-change rnd, with 6 sts between eyes. Close hole at back of head. If you prefer, sew or glue black felt circles (patt on page 75) for eyes, or use CC1 to make French knots (page 71). Embroider eyebrows with CC1 above eyes using a lazy daisy st (page 71). Fold nostrils in half and sew ends tog to form a teardrop shape. Attach nostrils to front of muzzle with 1 or 2 sts between them. Cut 2 ear patches (patt on page 75) from off-white felt, and sew or glue patches to RS of ears.

Attach narrow ends of ears to sides of head 3 rnds above eyes.

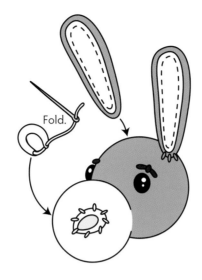

❷ Cut 1 belly patch (patt on page 75) from off-white felt. Attach patch to belly of body with either running st (page 71) or washable fabric glue. Pin and attach larger open edge of neck to top of smaller, tapered end of body. Attach head to open end of neck and stuff neck before closing seam. Attach legs halfway up sides of body. Attach open edge of tail to back of body.

❸ Cut 30 to 35 pieces of CC1, 4" long. Using fringe technique (page 73), attach to top of head and down back of neck. Cut 10 to 12 pieces, 4" long, and attach them to end of tail. Use tapestry needle to separate yarn strands and scissors to trim to desired length.

❹ To keep legs from splaying out, attach yarn to inside surface of one leg, pass yarn through body to inside surface of opposite leg, then back again through body to starting point. Pull gently to draw legs close to body. To form hoof shape, use CC1 and a tapestry needle, loop a long st of yarn from top of foot in back to bottom center of foot 2 or 3 times, pulling tightly as you sew. Rep on other 3 feet.

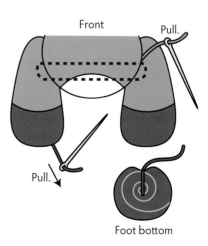

Sheep

No self-respecting yarn farmer could be without her flock of woolly friends! You can give your sheep and lambs all kinds of fun-looking wool coats by crocheting thickly textured yarns directly to the surface of the animals' bodies that might otherwise be too difficult to crochet with outright.

SHEEP

Skill Level: ◼◼◻◻

Finished Size: Approx 4½" tall and 5" long

Materials

Yarns:

MC   Approx 40 yds of worsted-weight yarn in white (4)

CC1   Approx 60 yds of worsted-weight yarn in dark gray (4)

CC2   Approx 30 yds of super bulky-weight yarn in white (6)

Approx 5 yds of worsted-weight yarn in black (4)

Notions:

Size G-6 (4 mm) and size J-10 (6 mm) crochet hook

8 mm or 9 mm black plastic eyes with safety backings *OR* small piece of black craft felt (if not using plastic eyes)

Sewing needle and black thread for sewing felt eyes

Tapestry needle

Stuffing

Stitch markers to indicate beginning of rounds (optional)

Color Variations for Sheep

For black, gray, and brown sheep, match the MC yarn and CC2 yarn as closely as possible. Dark-gray yarn is used for faces instead of black so that black eyes (felt, yarn, or plastic) will be easy to see on the face.

Use G hook throughout, except where noted.

Head

Using CC1, loosely ch 7.

Rnd 1: Starting in second ch from hook and working in back ridge loops, sc 5, sc 5 in back ridge loop of next ch. Rotate ch so front loops are facing up. Starting in next ch and working in front loops of ch, sc 4, sc 4 in next ch. (18 sts)

Rnd 2: Sc 2 in next st, sc 4, sc 2 in each of next 5 sts, sc 4, sc 2 in each of next 4 sts. (28 sts)

Rnds 3–6: Sc 28.

Rnd 7: *Sc 5, sc2tog; rep from * 3 more times. (24 sts)

Rnd 8: *Sc 2, sc2tog; rep from * 5 more times. (18 sts)

Rnds 9–11: Sc 18.

Rnd 12: *Sc 1, sc2tog; rep from * 5 more times. (12 sts)

Rnd 13: *Sc 1, sc2tog; rep from * 3 more times. (8 sts)

Stuff head.

Fasten off, leaving a long tail. Close up hole unless using plastic eyes.

Body

Using MC, make an 8-st adjustable ring (page 68).

Rnd 1: Sc 2 in each st around. (16 sts)

Rnd 2: *Sc 3, sc 2 in next st; rep from * 3 more times. (20 sts)

Rnd 3: *Sc 1, sc 2 in next st; rep from * 9 more times. (30 sts)

Rnds 4–8: Sc 30.

Rnd 9: *Sc 1, sc2tog; rep from * 9 more times. (20 sts)

Rnd 10: Sc 20.

Rnd 11: *Sc 3, sc2tog; rep from * 3 more times. (16 sts)

Rnd 12: Sc2tog 8 times. (8 sts)

Stuff body.

Fasten off, close up hole, and weave in end.

Legs

Make 4.

Using CC1, make a 6-st adjustable ring.

Rnd 1: Sc 3, sc 2 in next st, sc 3 in next st, sc 2 in next st. (10 sts)

Rnd 2: Sc 3, sc 2 in each of next 7 sts. (17 sts)

Rnd 3: In bl, sc 17.

Rnds 4 and 5: Sc 17.

Rnd 6: In bl, sc 1, sc2tog 8 times. (9 sts)

Rnds 7–10: Sc 9.

Change to CC2 and J crochet hook.

Rnd 11: In fl, hdc 9.

Stuff leg, and fasten off. Flatten seam and sew closed, leaving a long tail.

Tail

Using CC2 and J crochet hook, make a 4-st adjustable ring.

Fasten off, leaving a long tail.

Ears

Make 2.

Using CC1, loosely ch 6.

Starting in second ch from hook and working in back ridge loops, sc 2, hdc 2, dc 5 in back ridge loop of next ch. Rotate ch so front loops are facing up. Starting in next ch and working in front loops of ch, hdc 2, sc 2. Sl st at top of ch and fasten off.

Nostrils

Using CC1, loosely ch 16.

Sl st in 8th ch from hook, sk 7 sts and sl st in next ch. The 2 big loops will form the nostrils.

Fasten off, leaving a long tail.

Assembly

❶ Install plastic eyes to front of head between rnds 8 and 9, with 2 sts between eyes. Close hole at top of head. If you prefer, sew or glue black felt circles (patt on page 75) for eyes, or use black to make French knots (page 71). Using CC2 and J hook, attach

yarn at top of head and, following spiral of rounds, hdc onto surface (page 70) of head for 2 or 3 rnds. Position loops of nostrils in a V shape to front of head 1 rnd below eyes. Attach nostrils. Using black, draw long sts in a Y shape to front of face working directly over nostrils. With black, embroider eyebrows above eyes using lazy daisy st (page 71). Attach tapered end of ears to sides of head.

❷ Using CC2 and J hook, attach yarn to one end of body and loosely sc onto surface of entire body following spiral pattern of sts.

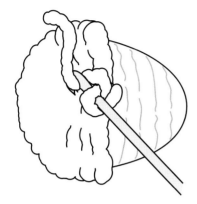

❸ Sew head to smaller end of body. Sew white portions of legs halfway up sides of body. Sew tail to back of body.

❹ To keep legs from splaying out, attach CC2 yarn to inside surface of one leg, pass yarn through body to inside surface of opposite leg, then back again through body to starting point. Pull gently to draw legs close to body. To form hooves, use CC1 yarn and a tapestry needle, draw and loop a long st of yarn from middle of foot in front to middle of foot in back, 2 or 3 times, pulling tightly as you sew. Rep on other 3 feet.

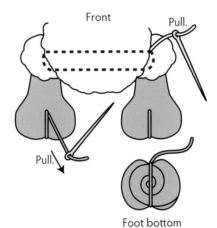

Front

Pull.

Pull.

Foot bottom

LAMB

Skill Level: ◼◼◻◻

Finished Size: Approx 2½" tall and 4" long

Materials

Yarns:

MC Approx 50 yds of worsted-weight yarn in white (4)

CC1 Approx 30 yds of worsted-weight yarn in dark gray (4)

CC2 Approx 25 yds of super bulky-weight yarn in white (6)

Approx 5 yds of worsted-weight yarn in black (4)

Notions:

Size G-6 (4 mm) and size J-10 (6 mm) crochet hooks

6 or 8 mm black plastic eyes with safety backings *OR* small piece of black craft felt (if not using plastic eyes)

Sewing needle and black thread for sewing felt eyes

Tapestry needle

Stuffing

Stitch markers to indicate beginning of rounds (optional)

Use G hook throughout, except where noted.

Head and Body

Using CC1, make an 8-st adjustable ring (page 68).

Rnd 1: Sc 2 in each st around. (16 sts)

Rnd 2: *Sc 3, sc 2 in next st; rep from * 3 more times. (20 sts)

Rnd 3: *Sc 1, sc 2 in next st; rep from * 9 more times. (30 sts)

Rnd 4: Sc 30.

Rnd 5: *Sc 1, sc2tog; rep from * 9 more times. (20 sts)

Rnd 6: *Sc 3, sc2tog; rep from * 3 more times. (16 sts)

Rnd 7: Sc2tog 8 times. (8 sts)

Lightly stuff head. If using plastic eyes, install them between rnds 1 and 2 with 2 or 3 sts between eyes. Finish stuffing head. Change to MC.

Rnd 8: Sc 2 in each st around. (16 sts)

Rnd 9: Sc 16.

Rnd 10: *Sc 7, sc 2 in next st; rep from * 1 more time. (18 sts)

Rnd 11: Sc 18.

Rnd 12: *Sc 5, sc 2 in next st; rep from * 2 more times. (21 sts)

Rnd 13: Sc 21.

Rnd 14: *Sc 6, sc 2 in next st; rep from * 2 more times. (24 sts)

Rnd 15: Sc2tog 12 times. (12 sts)
Stuff body.

Rnd 16: Sc2tog 6 times. (6 sts)
Fasten off. Close up hole and weave in end.

Legs

Make 4.
Using MC, make a 6-st adjustable ring.

Rnd 1: Sc 2 in each st around. (12 sts)

Rnd 2: Sc 12.

Rnd 3: Sc2tog 6 times. (6 sts)

Rnd 4: Sc 6.
Stuff and fasten off, leaving a long tail.

Tail

Using CC2 and J hook, loosely ch 3, sl st in third st from hook. Fasten off, leaving a long tail.

Ears

Make 2.
Using CC1, loosely ch 6.
Starting in second ch from hook and working in back ridge loops, sc 2, hdc 2, dc 5 in back ridge loop of next ch. Rotate ch so front loops are facing up. Starting in next ch and working in front loops of ch, hdc 2, sc 2. Sl st at top of ch and fasten off.

Assembly

❶ If not using plastic safety eyes, sew or glue black felt circles (patt on page 75) for eyes, or use black to make French knots (page 71) on front of head between rnds 1 and 2 with 2 or 3 sts between eyes. Using black, sew 2 short sts above each eye for eyebrows, and embroider a Y shape to front of face for lip cleft and nose. Pull firmly while sewing lip cleft to form 2 cheeks. Using CC2 and J hook, attach yarn at top of head and hdc onto surface (page 70) of head in a spiral path until

woolly patch measures about 1" across. Attach tapered end of ears to sides of head.

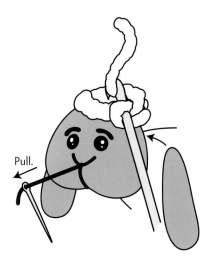

Pull.

❷ Using CC2 and J hook, attach yarn at back of body and loosely sc onto surface of entire body following spiral pattern of sts until you reach head. Fasten off and weave in end.

❸ Sew open edges of stuffed legs to bottom of body. Sew tail to back of body.

Alpaca

Alpacas come in such a lovely variety of colors, it might be hard to decide what color to make first. Don't forget to give yours a crazy haircut before you let it loose on your farm!

Skill Level: ◼◼◻◻◻   **Finished Size:** Approx 7" tall and 4½" long

Materials

Yarns: All yarns are worsted weight (4)

MC Approx 125 yds in medium brown

CC1 Approx 15 yds in dark brown

CC2 Approx 5 yds in cream

Approx 2 yds in black

Notions:

Size G-6 (4 mm) crochet hook

9 mm black plastic eyes with safety backings

Small piece of black craft felt (if not using plastic eyes)

Sewing needle and black thread for sewing felt eyes

Tapestry needle

Stuffing

Stitch markers to indicate beginning of rounds (optional)

Making a Baby Alpaca or "Cria"

For a cria, use DK-weight yarn, a size E-4 (3.5 mm) hook, size 6 mm plastic eyes with safety backings, and omit the nostril portion of the pattern. The little cria will be approx 6" tall and 3½" long.

Body, Neck, and Head

Using MC, make an 8-st adjustable ring (page 68).

Rnd 1: Sc 2 in each st around. (16 sts)

Rnd 2: *Sc 3, sc 2 in next st; rep from * 3 more times. (20 sts)

Rnd 3: *Sc 1, sc 2 in next st; rep from * 9 more times. (30 sts)

Rnds 4–8: Sc 30.

Rnd 9: *Sc 1, sc2tog; rep from * 9 more times. (20 sts)

Rnd 10: Sc 20.

Rnd 11: Hdc 5, *sc 3, sc2tog; rep from * 2 more times. (17 sts)

Rnd 12: Hdc 6, sc 3, sc2tog, sl st 1, sc2tog, sc 3. (15 sts)

Rnds 13–15: Hdc 6, in fl, sl st 9. (15 sts)

Rnds 16 and 17: Sc 15.

Rnd 18: *Sc 3, sc2tog; rep from * 2 more times. (12 sts)

Rnds 19–23: Sc 12.

Stuff body and neck.

Rnd 24: Sc 2 in each st around. (24 sts)

Rnd 25: *Sc 2, sc 2 in next st; rep from * 7 more times. (32 sts)

Rnds 26 and 27: Sc 32.

Rnd 28: *Sc 2, sc2tog; rep from * 7 more times. (24 sts)

Rnds 29–32: Sc 24.

Rnd 33: Sc2tog 12 times. (12 sts) Stuff head.

Rnd 34: *Sc 1, sc2tog; rep from * 3 more times. (8 sts)

Fasten off, leaving a long tail. Close up hole unless using plastic eyes.

Muzzle

Using CC2, make a 6-st adjustable ring.

Rnd 1: *Sc 1, sc 2 in next st; rep from * 2 more times. (9 sts)

Rnd 2: *Sc 2, sc 2 in next st; rep from * 2 more times. (12 sts)

Rnd 3: Sc 12.

Rnd 4: *Sc 2, sc2tog; rep from * 2 more times. (9 sts)

Stuff and fasten off, leaving a long tail.

Ears

Make 2.

Using MC, loosely ch 5.

Starting in second ch from hook and working in back ridge loops, sc 2, hdc 1, dc 5 in back ridge loop of next ch. Rotate ch so front loops are facing up. Starting in next ch and working in front loops of ch, hdc 1, sc 2. Fasten off and weave in end.

Legs

Make 4.

Using CC1, make a 6-st adjustable ring.

Rnd 1: *Sc 1, sc 2 in next st; rep from * 2 more times. (9 sts)

Rnd 2: *Sc 1, sc2tog; rep from * 2 more times. (6 sts)

Change to MC.

Rnd 3: In fl, sc 2 in each st around. (12 sts)

Rnd 4: In bl, *sc 1, sc 2 in next st; rep from * 5 more times. (18 sts)

Rnds 5–7: Sc 18.

Rnd 8: Sc2tog 9 times. (9 sts)

Rnds 9 and 10: Sc 9.

Stuff leg.

Rnd 11: Sc 1, sc2tog 4 times. (5 sts)

Fasten off. Flatten seam and sew closed, leaving a long tail.

Tail

Using MC, make a 6-st adjustable ring.

Rnd 1: Sc 2 in each st around. (12 sts)

Rnds 2 and 3: Sc 12.

Rnd 4: Sc2tog 6 times. (6 sts)

Fasten off, leaving a long tail. Do not stuff.

Nostrils

Skip if making cria.

Using CC2, loosely ch 16. Sl st in 8th ch from hook, sk 7 sts and sl st in next ch. The 2 big loops will form nostrils.

Fasten off, leaving a long tail.

Assembly

❶ Attach open end of muzzle to front of head and stuff. Install plastic eyes above muzzle with 2 or 3 sts between eyes. Close hole at top of head. If you prefer, sew or glue black felt circles (patt on page 75) for eyes, or use black to make French knots (page 71). Embroider eyebrows with black above eyes using a lazy daisy st (page 71). Attach ears to top

corners of head above eyebrows. *For worsted-weight alpaca,* position nostrils in a V shape to front of muzzle. Attach nostrils. Using black, make a long st in a Y shape to front of face working directly over nostrils. *For DK-weight alpaca,* omit nostrils and use black to embroider a Y shape to front of face for lip cleft and nose

Alpaca

Cria

4 To keep legs from splaying out, attach MC to inside surface of one leg, pass yarn through body to inside surface of opposite leg, then back again through body to starting point. Pull gently to draw legs close to body.

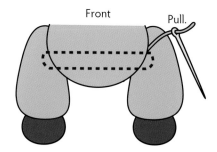

2 Sew legs halfway up sides of body. Sew tail to back of body. Using MC, make a few stitches between base of neck at back of body to help straighten up neck if needed.

3 Cut 15 to 20 pieces of MC, 4" long, and attach to top of head between ears using fringe technique (page 73). Use tapestry needle to separate yarn strands and scissors to trim to desired length.

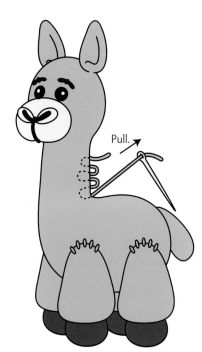

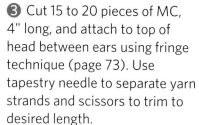

Goat

You won't find this billy goat sniffing around the trash pile for cans and old tires. Not when the farm has yummy things like tomatoes, pumpkins, and corn lying around in the field, just begging to be sampled!

Skill Level: ■■☐☐   **Finished Size:** Approx 5½" tall and 4½" long

Materials

Yarns: All yarns are worsted weight (4)

MC Approx 125 yds in white

CC1 Approx 25 yds in charcoal

CC2 Approx 20 yds in wheat

Approx 3 yds in black

Approx 1 yd of DK-weight in yellow (if making kid)

Notions:

Size G-6 (4 mm) crochet hook

8 mm or 9 mm black plastic eyes with safety backings *OR* small piece of black craft felt (if not using plastic eyes)

Sewing needle and black thread for sewing felt eyes

Tapestry needle

Stuffing

Stitch markers to indicate beginning of rounds (optional)

Note: Use MC throughout, except where noted.

Making a "Kid" Goat

To make a kid goat, use DK-weight yarn, a size D-3 (3.25 mm) hook, 9 mm eyes, and omit the nostril portion of the pattern. The kid will be approximately 4" tall and 4¼" long. Use DK-weight yellow for the stubs on the kid's head.

Head

Make a 6-st adjustable ring (page 68).

Rnd 1: Sc 2 in each st around. (12 sts)

Rnd 2: *Sc 2, sc 2 in next st; rep from * 3 more times. (16 sts)

Rnds 3–6: Sc 16.

Rnd 7: *Sc 7, sc 2 in next st; rep from * 1 more time. (18 sts)

Rnds 8 and 9: Sc 18.

Rnd 10: *Sc 5, sc 2 in next st; rep from * 2 more times. (21 sts)

Rnds 11 and 12: Sc 21.

Rnd 13: *Sc 6, sc 2 in next st; rep from * 2 more times. (24 sts)

Rnd 14: Sc2tog 12 times. (12 sts) Stuff head.

Rnd 15: *Sc 1, sc2tog; rep from * 3 more times. (8 sts)

Fasten off, leaving a long tail. Close up hole unless using plastic eyes.

Body

Make an 8-st adjustable ring.

Rnd 1: Sc 2 in each st around. (16 sts)

Rnd 2: *Sc 3, sc 2 in next st; rep from * 3 more times. (20 sts)

Rnd 3: *Sc 1, sc 2 in next st; rep from * 9 more times. (30 sts)

Rnds 4–8: Sc 30.

Rnd 9: *Sc 1, sc2tog; rep from * 9 more times. (20 sts)

Rnd 10: Sc 20.

Rnd 11: *Sc 3, sc2tog; rep from * 3 more times. (16 sts)

Rnd 12: Sc 16.

Rnd 13: Sc2tog 8 times. (8 sts) Stuff body.

Rnd 14: *Sc 2, sc2tog; rep from * 4 more times. (6 sts)

Fasten off, close up hole, and weave in end.

Nostrils

Skip if making kid.

Loosely ch 16. Sl st in 8th ch from hook, sk 7 sts and sl st in next ch. The 2 big loops will form nostrils.

Fasten off, leaving a long tail.

Ears

Make 2.

Loosely ch 6.

Starting in second ch from hook and working in back ridge loops, sc 2, hdc 2, dc 5 in back ridge loop of next ch. Rotate ch so front loops are facing up. Starting in next st and working in front loops of ch, hdc 2, sc 2. Sl st at top of ch and fasten off, leaving a long tail.

Tail

Make a 6-st adjustable ring.

Rnd 1: Sc 2 in each st around. (12 sts)

Rnds 2 and 3: Sc 12.

Rnd 4: Sc2tog 6 times. (6 sts)

Stuff and fasten off, leaving a long tail.

Legs

Make 4.

Using CC1, make a 6-st adjustable ring.

Rnd 1: Sc 3, sc 2 in next st, sc 3 in next st, sc 2 in next st. (10 sts)

Rnd 2: Sc 3, sc 2 in each of next 7 sts. (17 sts)

Rnd 3: In bl, sc 17.

Rnds 4 and 5: Sc 17.

Change to MC.

Rnd 6: Sc 1, sc2tog 8 times. (9 sts)

Rnds 7–10: Sc 9.

Stuff leg.

Rnd 11: Sc 1, sc2tog 4 times. (5 sts)

Fasten off. Flatten seam and sew closed, leaving a long tail.

Large Horns

Skip if making kid.

Make 2.

Using CC2, make a 6-st adjustable ring.

Rnd 1: In bl, sc 6.

Rnds 2–4: Sc 6.

Rnd 5: *Sc 1, sc2tog; rep from * 1 more time. (4 sts)

Rnd 6: Sc 4.

Rnd 7: Sk 1, sl st 1.

Fasten off, leaving a long tail.

Kid Horns

Make 2.

Using DK-weight yellow, make a 5-st adjustable ring.

Sc 5.

Fasten off, leaving a long tail.

Assembly

❶ Install plastic eyes to sides of head between rnds 8 and 9 with 6 sts between eyes. Close hole at back of head. If you prefer, sew or glue black felt circles (patt on page 75) for eyes, or use black to make French knots (page 71). With black, embroider eyebrows above eyes using lazy daisy st (page 71). *For goat,* position nostrils in a V shape at front of muzzle. Attach nostrils. Using black, make a long st in a Y shape to front of face working directly over nostrils.

For kid, omit nostrils and use black to embroider a Y shape to front of face for lip cleft and nose.

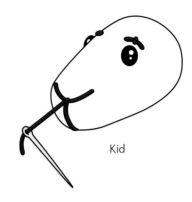

Kid

❷ *For goat,* attach open end of horns to top of head, 1 or 2 rnds behind eyebrows. Using leftover yarn tail at top of horn, sew a running st down back of horn from tip to base and pull gently to curve horn. *For kid,* attach open end of horn stubs to top of head above eyebrows. Secure and weave in end. *For both,* sew ears to corners of head 1 rnd behind horns. Using CC1, cut 5 pieces, 4" long, for goat, and 2 pieces, 2" long, for kid. Using fringe technique (page 73), attach to chin. Use tapestry needle to separate yarn strands and scissors to trim and shape beard.

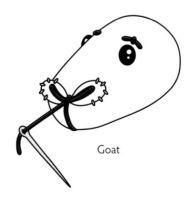

Goat

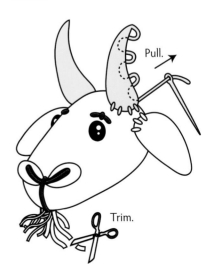

Pull.

Trim.

3 Attach head to top of larger, rounder end of body. Attach legs halfway up sides of body. Attach open edge of tail to back of body.

of opposite leg, then back again through body to starting point. Pull gently to draw legs close to body. To form hooves, use CC1 and a tapestry needle, loop a long st of yarn from top of foot in front to top of foot in back 2 or 3 times, pulling tightly as you sew. Rep on other 3 feet.

4 To keep legs from splaying out, attach yarn to inside surface of one leg, pass yarn through body to inside surface

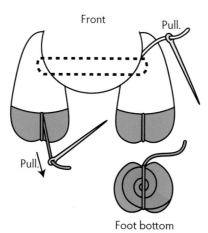

Front

Pull.

Pull.

Foot bottom

Old English Sheepdog

With so many unruly, troublemaking sheep on the farm, it's a good thing you'll have a friendly Old English sheepdog to keep them in line. Be prepared to spend some time attaching all the fringe needed to give your pooch his signature thick and fuzzy coat.

Skill Level: ◼◼◻◻   **Finished Size:** Approx 4" tall and 4½" long

Materials

Yarns: All yarns are DK weight 🧶**3**

MC   Approx 75 yds in white

CC   Approx 75 yds in gray heather

Approx 7 yds in black

Notions:

Size D-3 (3.25 mm) crochet hook

6 mm black plastic eyes with safety backings

Small piece of black craft felt (if not using plastic eyes)

Sewing needle and black thread for sewing felt eyes

Tapestry needle

Stuffing

Stitch markers to indicate beginning of rounds (optional)

Note: Use MC throughout, except where noted.

Muzzle

Make an 8-st adjustable ring (page 68).

Rnd 1: Sc 2 in each st around. (16 sts)

Rnd 2: *Sc 7, sc 2 in next st; rep from * 1 more time. (18 sts)

Rnd 3: *Sc 4, sc2tog; rep from * 2 more times. (15 sts)

Fasten off, leaving a long tail.

Head

Make a 6-st adjustable ring.

Rnd 1: Sc 2 in each st around. (12 sts)

Rnd 2: *Sc 1, sc 2 in next st; rep from * 5 more times. (18 sts)

Rnd 3: *Sc 5, sc 2 in next st; rep from * 2 more times. (21 sts)

Rnd 4: *Sc 6, sc 2 in next st; rep from * 2 more times. (24 sts)

Rnd 5: *Sc 5, sc 2 in next st; rep from * 3 more times. (28 sts)

Rnds 6 and 7: Sc 8, hdc 12, sc 8. (28 sts)

Rnd 8: Sc2tog 4 times, sc 12, sc2tog 4 times. (20 sts)

Rnd 9: *Sc 2, sc2tog; rep from * 4 more times. (15 sts)

Rnd 10: *Sc 3, sc2tog; rep from * 2 more times. (12 sts)

Stuff head.

Rnd 11: *Sc 1, sc2tog; rep from * 3 more times. (8 sts)

Fasten off, leaving a long tail. Close up hole unless using plastic eyes.

Body

Starting with MC, make an 8-st adjustable ring.

Rnd 1: Sc 2 in each st around. (16 sts)

Rnd 2: *Sc 3, sc 2 in next st; rep from * 3 more times. (20 sts)

Rnd 3: *Sc 1, sc 2 in next st; rep from * 9 more times. (30 sts)

Rnds 4 and 5: Sc 30.

Change to CC.

Rnds 6-8: Sc 30.

Rnd 9: *Sc 1, sc2tog; rep from * 9 more times. (20 sts)

Rnd 10: Sc 20.

Rnd 11: *Sc 3, sc2tog; rep from * 3 more times. (16 sts)

Rnd 12: Sc 16.

Rnd 13: Sc2tog 8 times. (8 sts)

Stuff body.

Rnd 14: *Sc 2, sc2tog; rep from * 1 more time. (6 sts)

Fasten off, close up hole, and weave in end.

Ears

Make 2.

Loosely ch 4.

Row 1: Starting second ch from hook, sc 1, sc 2 in next st, sc 1. Ch 1, turn. (4 sts)

Rows 2–6: Sk first ch, sc 4. Ch 1, turn. (4 sts)

Row 7: Sk first ch, sc2tog 2 times. Ch 1, turn. (2 sts)

Row 8: Sk first ch, sc2tog. (1 st)

Sl st around edge of ear until you reach opposite side of row 8. Fasten off, leaving a long tail.

Nose

Using black, make a 7-st adjustable ring.

Sl st 7.

Fasten off, leaving a long tail.

Front Legs

Make 2.

Make a 6-st adjustable ring.

Rnd 1: Sc 1, sc 2 in next st, hdc 2 in each of next 2 sts, sc 2 in next st, sc 1. (10 sts)

Rnd 2: Sc 2, hdc 6, sc 2. (10 sts)

Rnd 3: Sc 3, sc2tog 2 times, sc 3. (8 sts)

Rnd 4: *Sc 1, sc 2 in next st; rep from * 3 more times. (12 sts)

Rnds 5 and 6: Sc 12.

Rnd 7: *Sc 2, sc 2 in next st; rep from * 3 more times. (16 sts)

Rnd 8: Sc 16.

Rnd 9: *Sc 2, sc2tog; rep from * 3 more times. (12 sts)

Rnd 10: Sc 12.

Stuff leg.

Rnd 11: Sc2tog 6 times. (6 sts)

Fasten off. Flatten seam and sew closed, leaving a long tail.

Back Legs

Make 2.

Starting with MC, make a 6-st adjustable ring.

Rnd 1: Sc 1, sc 2 in next st, hdc 2 in each of next 2 sts, sc 2 in next st, sc 1. (10 sts)

Rnd 2: Sc 2, hdc 6, sc 2. (10 sts)

Rnd 3: Sc 3, sc2tog 2 times, sc 3. (8 sts)

Change to CC.

Rnd 4: *Sc 1, sc 2 in next st; rep from * 3 more times. (12 sts)

Rnds 5 and 6: Sc 12.

Rnd 7: *Sc 2, sc 2 in next st; rep from * 3 more times. (16 sts)

Rnd 8: Sc 16.

Rnd 9: *Sc 2, sc2tog; rep from * 3 more times. (12 sts)

Rnd 10: Sc 12.

Stuff leg.

Rnd 11: Sc2tog 6 times. (6 sts)

Fasten off. Flatten seam and sew closed, leaving a long tail.

Tail

Starting with MC, make a 4-st adjustable ring.

Rnd 1: *Sc 1, sc 2 in next st; rep from * 1 more time. (6 sts)

Rnd 2: *Sc 2, sc 2 in next st; rep from * 1 more time. (8 sts)

Change to CC.

Rnd 3: *Sc 3, sc 2 in next st; rep from * 1 more time. (10 sts)

Rnd 4: *Sc 4, sc 2 in next st; rep from * 1 more time. (12 sts)

Rnd 5: Sc 12.

Lightly stuff.

Rnd 6: Sc2tog 6 times. (6 sts)

Fasten off, leaving a long tail.

Assembly

❶ Position head with 8-st opening at back of head and rows of hdc, from rnds 6 and 7, facing up. Sew open edge of

muzzle to lower front half of head and stuff before closing seam. Install plastic eyes just above muzzle with 1 or 2 sts between eyes. Close hole at back of head. If you prefer, sew or glue black felt circles (patt on page 75) for eyes, or use black to make French knots (page 71). With black, embroider eyebrows above eyes using lazy daisy st (page 71). Sew open edge of nose to upper front half of muzzle. With black and a tapestry needle, loop a long st of yarn out from back of chin to base of nose and back out chin again 1 or 2 times, pulling tightly to form lip cleft. Sew flat edges of ears to top corners of head 2 or 3 rnds behind eyebrows. After attaching, ears can be posed up (as in photo on page 46) or down as shown here.

Pull.

❷ Attach head to top of larger, rounder white portion of body. Attach legs halfway up sides of body. Attach open edge of tail to back of body.

3 To keep legs from splaying out, attach yarn to inside surface of one leg, pass yarn through body to inside surface of opposite leg, then back again through body to starting point. Pull gently to draw legs close to body.

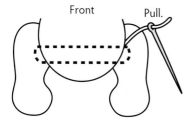

4 Using fringe technique (page 73), cut as many 4"-long pieces of MC and CC as needed to cover respective areas of white and gray on body and head excluding first 3 rnds of feet, tail, ears, black nose, belly surface, and immediate area around eyes. Use tapestry needle to separate yarn strands and scissors to trim and shape coat. Keep yarn long

directly in front of eyes for that classic sheepdog look.

Front leg and back leg detail

Tail detail

Cat

Every farm needs a cat to help keep the small critters from nibbling the goodies being stored in the barn and silo. This little tabby is particularly happy to be hanging out at a farm with such a surplus of yarn balls.

Skill Level: ◼◼◻◻   **Finished Size:** Approx 3½" tall and 4½" long

Materials

Yarns: All yarns are DK weight (3)

MC   Approx 60 yds in orange

CC   Approx 20 yds in white

Approx 7 yds in black

Approx 1 yd in pink

Notions:

Size D-3 (3.25 mm) crochet hook

6 mm black plastic eyes with safety backings *OR* small piece of black craft felt (if not using plastic eyes)

Small pieces of white and dark-red craft felt for belly and stripes

Sewing needle and thread to match felt

Tapestry needle

Stuffing

Stitch markers to indicate beginning of rounds (optional)

Muzzle

Using CC, make an 8-st adjustable ring (page 68).

Rnd 1: Sc 2 in each st around. (16 sts)

Rnd 2: *Sc 7, sc 2 in next st; rep from * 1 more time. (18 sts)

Rnd 3: *Sc 4, sc2tog; rep from * 2 more times. (15 sts)

Fasten off, leaving a long tail.

Head

Using MC, loosely ch 7.

Rnd 1: Starting in second ch from hook and working in back ridge loops, sc 5, sc 5 in back ridge loop of next ch. Rotate ch so front loops are facing up. Starting in next ch and working in front loops of ch, sc 4, sc 4 in next ch. (18 sts)

Rnd 2: Sc 2 in next st, sc 4, sc 2 in each of next 5 sts, sc 4, sc 2 in each of next 4 sts. (28 sts)

Rnds 3–6: Sc 28.

Rnd 7: *Sc 5, sc2tog; rep from * 3 more times. (24 sts)

Rnd 8: *Sc 2, sc2tog; rep from * 5 more times. (18 sts)

Rnds 9 and 10: Sc 18.

Rnd 11: *Sc 1, sc2tog; rep from * 5 more times. (12 sts)

Rnd 12: *Sc 1, sc2tog; rep from * 3 more times. (8 sts)

Stuff head.

Fasten off, leaving a long tail. Close up hole unless using plastic eyes.

Body

Using MC, make an 8-st adjustable ring.

Rnd 1: Sc 2 in each st around. (16 sts)

Rnd 2: *Sc 3, sc 2 in next st; rep from * 3 more times. (20 sts)

Rnd 3: *Sc 1, sc 2 in next st; rep from * 9 more times. (30 sts)

Rnds 4–8: Sc 30.

Rnd 9: *Sc 1, sc2tog; rep from * 9 more times. (20 sts)

Rnd 10: Sc 20.

Rnd 11: *Sc 3, sc2tog; rep from * 3 more times. (16 sts)

Rnd 12: Sc 16.

Rnd 13: Sc2tog 8 times. (8 sts)

Stuff body.

Rnd 14: *Sc 2, sc2tog; rep from * 1 more time. (6 sts)

Fasten off, close up hole, and weave in end.

Ears

Make 2.

Using MC, make a 5-st adjustable ring. Ch 1, turn.

Sk first ch, sc 1, hdc 1, (hdc 1, dc 1, hdc 1) in next st, hdc 1, sc 1. (7 sts)

Fasten off, leaving a long tail.

Nose

Using pink, make a 4-st adjustable ring.

Fasten off. *DO NOT* join last st to first st (in order to create a small semicircle shape)

Legs

Make 4.

Starting with CC, make a 6-st adjustable ring.

Rnd 1: Sc 3, sc 2 in next st, sc 3 in next st, sc 2 in next st. (10 sts)

Rnd 2: Sc 3, sc 2 in each of next 7 sts. (17 sts)

Rnd 3: In bl, sc 17.

Rnds 4 and 5: Sc 17.

Change to MC.

Rnd 6: In bl, sc 1, sc2tog 8 times. (9 sts)

Rnds 7–10: Sc 9.

Stuff leg.

Rnd 11: Sc 1, sc2tog 4 times. (5 sts)

Fasten off. Flatten seam and sew closed, leaving a long tail.

Tail

Starting with CC, make a 4-st adjustable ring.

Rnd 1: *Sc 1, sc 2 in next st; rep from * 1 more time. (6 sts)

Rnd 2: *Sc 2, sc 2 in next st; rep from * 1 more time. (8 sts)

Change to MC.

Rnd 3: *Sc 3, sc 2 in next st; rep from * 1 more time. (10 sts)

Rnd 4: *Sc 4, sc 2 in next st; rep from * 1 more time. (12 sts)

Rnds 5 and 6: Sc 12.

Lightly stuff.

Rnd 7: *Sc 2, sc2tog; rep from * 2 more times. (9 sts)

Rnd 8: *Sc 1, sc2tog; rep from * 2 more times. (6 sts)

Fasten off, leaving a long tail.

Assembly

❶ Position head with opening at top. Sew open edge of muzzle to lower front half of head and stuff before closing seam. Install plastic eyes just above muzzle with 1 or 2 sts between eyes. Close hole at top of head. If you prefer, sew or glue black felt circles (patt on page 75) for eyes, or use black to make French knots (page 71). With black, embroider eyebrows above eyes using lazy daisy st (page 71). With round edge of nose facing down, sew nose to top of muzzle. With black and a tapestry needle, apply a long stitch of yarn from one corner of nose to the other to follow along bottom half of nose, then loop a long st of yarn out from back of chin to base of nose and back out chin again 1 or 2 times, pulling tightly to form lip cleft. Sew 3 short sts along edge of each cheek for whiskers. Sew flat edges of ears to sides of head 4 or 5 sts behind eyebrows.

❷ Attach head to top of smaller, tapered end of body. Attach legs halfway up sides of body. Attach open edge of tail to back of body.

❸ Using patts on page 75, cut 1 belly patch from white felt, and cut 2 small stripes, 3 medium stripes, and 2 large stripes from dark-red felt. With tapered end of belly patch facing front, attach with white thread and running st (page 71) or with washable fabric glue. Working from back of head to tail, pin 1 medium and 1 large stripe on back of head, 1 medium, 1 large, and 1 medium stripe along back, and 2 small stripes on tail. Attach with a running st and red thread or with washable fabric glue.

❹ Cut 10 to 12 pieces of MC, 4" long, and using fringe technique (page 73), attach to top of head and along edges of cheeks. Cut 2 pieces of CC, 4" long, and attach to chin. Use tapestry needle to separate yarn strands and scissors to trim to desired length.

Trim.

❺ To keep legs from splaying out, attach yarn to inside surface of one leg, pass yarn through body to inside surface of opposite leg, then back again through body to starting point. Pull gently to draw legs close to body. With black, form toes by looping yarn from rnd 1 around to rnd 5 on foot, and through foot back to rnd 1 again, 2 or 3 times, pulling tightly to form toes. Rep about 3 sts away from first set of loops. Rep on rem 3 feet.

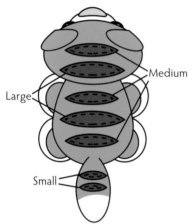

Medium

Large

Small

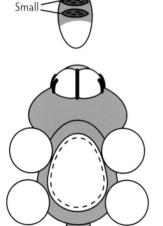

Front

Pull.

Pull.

Foot bottom

Mouse

While the farm cat is distracted by the stash of amazing yarn Farmer McDonald left lying around, these little mice can easily pop into the silo (or pantry) and help themselves to just a few nibbles here and there.

Skill Level: ■■□□ **Finished Size:** Sitting Mouse: Approx 1½" tall and 2¼" long
Walking Mouse: Approx 2¼" tall and 1½" long

Materials

Materials are enough for 2 mice.

Yarns: All yarns are DK weight [3]

MC Approx 30 yds in gray

CC Approx 10 yds in pink

Approx 3 yds in black

Notions:

Size E-4 (3.5 mm) crochet hook

4 mm or 5 mm black plastic eyes with safety backings *OR* small piece of black craft felt (if not using plastic eyes)

Sewing needle and black thread for sewing felt eyes

Tapestry needle

Stuffing

Stitch markers to indicate beginning of rounds (optional)

Note: There are two types of bodies. All other parts apply to both bodies.

Sitting Mouse Body

Using MC, make a 6-st adjustable ring (page 68).

Rnd 1: Sc 3, sc 2 in next st, sc 3 in next st, sc 2 in next st. (10 sts)

Rnd 2: Sc 3, sc 2 in each of next 7 sts. (17 sts)

Rnd 3: In bl, sc 17.

Rnds 4 and 5: Sc 17.

Rnd 6: Sc2tog, *sc 1, sc2tog; rep from * 4 more times. (11 sts)

Rnd 7: Sc 1, *sc 3, sc2tog; rep from * 1 more time. (9 sts)

Rnds 8-10: Sc 9.

Stuff body. Fasten off, leaving a long tail. Close up hole unless using plastic eyes.

Walking Mouse Body

Using MC, make a 6-st adjustable ring.

Rnd 1: Sc 3, sc 2 in next st, sc 3 in next st, sc 2 in next st. (10 sts)

Rnd 2: Sc 3, sc 2 in each of next 7 sts. (17 sts)

Rnds 3-5: Sc 17.

Rnd 6: Sc2tog, *sc 1, sc2tog; rep from * 4 more times. (11 sts)

Rnd 7: Sc 1, *sc 3, sc2tog; rep from * 1 more time. (9 sts)

Rnds 8-10: Sc 9.

Stuff body. Fasten off, leaving a long tail. Close up hole unless using plastic eyes.

Muzzle

Using MC, make a 6-st adjustable ring.

Sl st 6.

Fasten off, leaving a long tail.

Ears

Make 2.

Using MC, make an 8-st adjustable ring. *DO NOT* join.

Fasten off, leaving a long tail.

Paws

Make 4.

Using CC, make a 4-st adjustable ring.

Sl st in first st to join.

Fasten off, leaving a long tail.

Assembly

❶ Install plastic eyes between rnds 8 and 9 with 1 or 2 sts between eyes. Close hole at top of body. If you prefer, sew or glue black felt circles (patt on page 75) for eyes, or use black to make French knots (page 71). *For sitting mouse,* hold sitting body vertically and sew open end of muzzle to side of head directly below eyes. *For walking mouse,* lay walking body horizontally and sew open end of muzzle to front of head directly below eyes. Make 2 short sts above each eye for eyebrows.

❷ Using black, make a bulky French knot (bulk-up technique on page 72) on top front of muzzle for nose. Attach ears to head above eyebrows. Cut 1 piece of MC, 3" long. Using fringe technique (page 73), attach to top of head. Use tapestry needle to separate yarn strands and scissors to trim and shape hair.

❸ *For sitting mouse,* attach front paws flat to body 1 rnd below muzzle and back paws to bottom edge of body below rnd 3. *For walking mouse,* position paws at 4 corners of belly and sew in place. After securing paws on *both types of mice,* work 1 of the back-paw yarn tails out the back end of body for a mouse tail, tie a knot at end of tail, and trim excess yarn.

Sitting

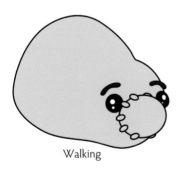

Walking

Trim.

Trim.

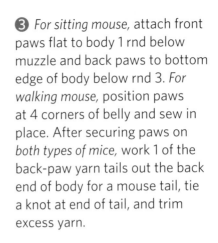

Farm Harvest

Pumpkins and apples and corn cobs, oh my! This bountiful mix of farm goodies will certainly keep the farmers busy from dawn to dusk. In between collecting eggs, milking cows, harvesting hay, and picking apples, hopefully they'll find time to do some crocheting as well.

Skill Level: ■■■□   **Finished Size:** varies

Materials

Yarns:

Worsted-weight yarn (4)

MC Approx 20 yds in yellow

DK-weight yarns (3)

A	Approx 15 yds in orange
B	Approx 10 yds in brown
C	Approx 10 yds in gray
D	Approx 10 yds in red
E	Approx 10 yds in yellow
F	Approx 10 yds in green
G	Approx 10 yds in dark red

Approx 5 yds in white

Approx 5 yds in light brown

Size D-3 (3.25 mm) crochet hook

Size E-4 (3.5 mm) crochet hook

Size G-6 (4 mm) crochet hook

Felt in various greens and white

Sewing needle and sewing thread in green, white, and dark red

Tapestry needle

Stuffing

Fabric glue (optional)

Stitch markers to indicate beginning of rounds (optional)

Hay Bundles

Use G hook.

Large Bundle

Using MC, make 6-st adjustable ring (page 68).

Rnd 1: Sc 2 in each st around. (12 sts)

Rnd 2: *Sc 1, sc 2 in next st; rep from * 5 more times. (18 sts)

Rnd 3: In bl, sc 18.

Rnds 4–6: Sc 18.

Rnd 7: *Sc 4, sc2tog; rep from * 2 more times. (15 sts)

Rnds 8 and 9: Sc 15.

Rnd 10: *Sc 3, sc2tog; rep from * 2 more times. (12 sts)

Rnds 11 and 12: Sc 12.

Stuff bundle.

Rnd 13: *Sc 1, sc2tog; rep from * 3 more times. (8 sts)

Rnd 14: Sc 2 in each st around. (16 sts)

Rnd 15: Sc2tog 8 times.

Finish stuffing bundle. Fasten off, leaving a long tail.

Assembly

Using 2 long strands of MC, folded in half and double threaded onto tapestry needle (page 74), attach at rnd 3 of bundle and loop long sts between rnd 3 and rnd 13, working all the way around bundle. Using 1 long strand of B, folded in half and double threaded, wrap yarn around rnd 13 about 5 or 6 times and fasten off. Cut 15 to 20 pieces of MC, 4" long. Using fringe technique (page 73), attach to bundle above B yarn. Use tapestry needle to separate yarn strands and use scissors to trim and shape.

Small Bundle

Using MC, make 6-st adjustable ring.

Rnd 1: Sc 2 in each st around. (12 sts)

Rnd 2: In bl, sc 12.

Rnds 3–9: Sc 12.

Rnd 10: *Sc 1, sc2tog; rep from * 3 more times. (8 sts)

Rnds 11 and 12: Sc 8.

Rnd 13: Sc 2 in each st around. (16 sts)

Rnd 14: In bl, sc2tog 8 times.

Stuff bundle. Fasten off, leaving a long tail.

Assembly

Using 2 long strands of MC, folded in half and double

threaded onto tapestry needle, attach at rnd 3 of bundle and loop long sts between rnd 2 and rnd 12 all the way around bundle. Using 1 long strand of B, folded in half and double threaded, wrap around rnd 12 about 5 or 6 times and fasten off. Cut and attach fringe to bundle above B as for large hay bundle.

Milk Pail

Use E hook.

Pail

Using C, make an 8-st adjustable ring.

Rnd 1: Sc 2 in each st around. (16 sts)

Rnd 2: In bl, sc 16.

Rnd 3: Sc 16.

Rnd 4: *Sc 7, sc 2 in next st; rep from * 1 more time. (18 sts)

Rnd 5: *Sc 8, sc 2 in next st; rep from * 1 more time. (20 sts)

Rnd 6: In bl, sc 20.

Rnd 7: *Sc 9, sc 2 in next st; rep from * 1 more time. (22 sts)

Rnd 8: *Sc 10, sc 2 in next st; rep from * 1 more time. (24 sts)

Rnd 9: Sc 24.

Rnd 10: FPsc 24.

Fasten off, leaving a long tail. Stretch out opening of pail to loosen up FPsc sts.

Milk

Using white, make an 8-st adjustable ring.

Rnd 1: Sc 2 in each st around. (16 sts)

Rnd 2: In bl, sc 16.

Rnd 3: Sc 16.

Rnd 4: *Sc 7, sc 2 in next st; rep from * 1 more time. (18 sts)

Rnd 5: *Sc 8, sc 2 in next st; rep from * 1 more time. (20 sts)

Rnd 6: Sc 20.

Rnd 7: In bl, sc2tog 10 times. (10 sts)

Stuff lightly.

Rnd 8: Sc2tog 5 times. (5 sts)

Fasten off, close up hole at bottom of milk piece, and weave in end.

Handle

Using B, loosely ch 20, starting in 2nd ch from hook, sl st 19. Fasten off, leaving a long tail.

Assembly

Cut a circle from white felt large enough to cover top of milk piece and sew or glue in place. Insert milk into pail and secure with a few stitches of white, or glue in place. Attach ends of handle to opposite sides of pail brim. Feel free to adjust handle size as needed.

Pumpkins

Use E hook.

Small Pumpkin

Using A, make a 6-st adjustable ring.

Rnd 1: Sc 2 in each st around. (12 sts)

Rnd 2: *Sc 1, sc 2 in next st; rep from * 5 more times. (18 sts)

Rnd 3: *Sc 2, sc 2 in next st; rep from * 5 more times. (24 sts)

Rnd 4: *Sc 3, sc 2 in next st; rep from * 5 more times. (30 sts)

Rnds 5–8: Sc 30.

Rnd 9: *Sc 3, sc2tog; rep from * 5 more times. (24 sts)

Rnd 10: *Sc 2, sc2tog; rep from * 5 more times. (18 sts)

Rnd 11: *Sc 1, sc2tog; rep from * 5 more times. (12 sts)

Stuff.

Rnd 12: Sc2tog 6 times. (6 sts)

Fasten off, leaving a long tail.

Large Pumpkin

Using A, make a 6-st adjustable ring.

Rnd 1: Sc 2 in each st around. (12 sts)

Rnd 2: *Sc 1, sc 2 in next st; rep from * 5 more times. (18 sts)

Rnd 3: *Sc 2, sc 2 in next st; rep from * 5 more times. (24 sts)

Rnd 4: *Sc 3, sc 2 in next st; rep from * 5 more times. (30 sts)

Rnd 5: *Sc 4, sc 2 in next st; rep from * 5 more times. (36 sts)

Rnd 6: *Sc 5, sc 2 in next st; rep from * 5 more times. (42 sts)

Rnds 7–11: Sc 42.

Rnd 12: *Sc 5, sc2tog; rep from * 5 more times. (36 sts)

Rnd 13: *Sc 4, sc2tog; rep from * 5 more times. (30 sts)

Rnd 14: *Sc 3, sc2tog; rep from * 5 more times. (24 sts)

Rnd 15: *Sc 2, sc2tog; rep from * 5 more times. (18 sts)

Rnd 16: *Sc 1, sc2tog; rep from * 5 more times. (12 sts)
Stuff.
Rnd 17: Sc2tog 6 times. (6 sts)
Fasten off, leaving a long tail.

Pumpkin Stem

Using B, loosely ch 7. Starting in second ch from hook, sc 2 in each of next 6 chs.

Assembly

Using tapestry needle and A, draw long stitches from top of pumpkin at center to bottom of pumpkin and up through center again 1 or 2 times. Pull tightly to cinch and crease pumpkin shell. Rep in 5 additional spots evenly spaced along shell to shape pumpkin. Sew stem to top of pumpkin. Using vine pattern on page 75, cut 1 or 2 vines from green felt. Use sewing needle and green thread to sew vine to base of pumpkin stem, allowing vine to hang loosely over side of pumpkin.

Apple

Use D hook.

Apple

Using D or F, make a 6-st adjustable ring.
Rnd 1: Sc 2 in each st around. (12 sts)
Rnd 2: Sc 12.

Rnd 3: *Sc 1, sc 2 in next st; rep from * 5 more times. (18 sts)
Rnds 4-6: Sc 18.
Rnd 7: *Sc 1, sc2tog; rep from * 5 more times. (12 sts)
Stuff.
Rnd 8: Sc2tog 6 times.
Fasten off. Close hole, leaving a long tail.

Stem

Using B, loosely ch 4. Starting in second ch from hook, sl st 3. Fasten off, leaving a long tail.

Assembly

Draw leftover yarn tail from apple down and out through middle of apple, pulling firmly to sink top of apple and secure shaping by fastening off at base of apple. Attach apple stem. Using leaf pattern on page 75, cut 1 leaf from green felt. Pinch one end of leaf tog and secure with a couple of sts before sewing leaf to base of apple stem with sewing needle and green thread.

Tomato

Using D hook and G, make a 6-st adjustable ring.
Rnd 1: Sc 2 in each st around. (12 sts)
Rnd 2: *Sc 1, sc 2 in next st; rep from * 5 more times. (18 sts)

Rnds 3-6: Sc 18.
Rnd 7: *Sc 1, sc2tog; rep from * 5 more times. (12 sts)
Stuff.
Rnd 8: Sc2tog 6 times.
Fasten off. Close hole, leaving a long tail.

Assembly

Draw leftover yarn tail from tomato up and down through middle of tomato 2 or 3 times, pulling firmly to draw top and bottom of tomato tog. Fasten off, and weave in end. Using stem star pattern on page 75, cut 1 star from green felt. Sew center of stem to top of tomato using sewing needle and green thread.

Carrot

Using D hook and A, make an 8-st adjustable ring.
Rnd 1: *Sc 3, sc 2 in next st; rep from * 1 more time. (10 sts)
Rnd 2: *Sc 4, sc 2 in next st; rep from * 1 more time. (12 sts)
Rnds 3 and 4: Sc 12.
Rnd 5: *Sc 2, sc2tog; rep from * 2 more times. (9 sts)
Rnds 6 and 7: Sc 9.
Stuff.
Rnd 8: *Sc 1, sc2tog; rep from * 2 more times. (6 sts)

Rnds 9 and 10: Sc 6.

Rnd 11: Sc2tog 3 times. (3 sts) Fasten off. Close hole and weave in end.

Assembly

Using carrot top pattern on page 75, cut 1 carrot top from green felt and fringe ends with sharp scissors where indicated on pattern. Use sewing needle and green thread to sew center of carrot leaf stem to top of carrot, then fold 2 sides of leaf shape tog and wrap sewing thread around stem of leaves 4 or 5 times. Fasten off. Muss up leafy fringe with your fingers.

Corn

Using D hook and E, make a 4-st adjustable ring.

Rnd 1: Sc 2 in each st around. (8 sts)

Rnd 2: *Sc 1, sc 2 in next st; rep from * 3 more times. (12 sts)

Rnds 3–8: *In bl, sc 1, in fl, sc 1; rep from * 5 more times. (12 sts)

Rnd 9: *Sc 1, sc2tog; rep from * 3 more times. (8 sts)

Stuff.

Rnd 10: *Sc 2, sc2tog; rep from * 1 more time. (6 sts)

Fasten off. Close hole and weave in end.

Assembly

Using corn leaf pattern on page 75, cut 4 leaves from green felt. Overlap 2 leaves slightly. Use sewing needle and green thread to sew bottom halves of leaves to bottom and back lower half of corn. Position 2 other leaves on sides of corn, taking care to overlap back 2 leaves and sew lower halves of side leaves to bottom and sides of corn.

Egg

Using D hook and white or light brown, make a 6-st adjustable ring.

Rnd 1: *Sc 1, sc 2 in next st; rep from * 2 more times. (9 sts)

Rnd 2: Sc 2 in each st around. (18 sts)

Rnds 35: Sc 18.

Rnd 6: *Sc 1, sc2tog; rep from * 5 more times. (12 sts)

Rnd 7: *Sc 2, sc2tog; rep from * 2 more times. (9 sts)

Stuff.

Rnd 8: *Sc 1, sc2tog; rep from * 2 more times. (6 sts)

Fasten off. Close hole and weave in end.

Basic Supplies

When it comes to materials, always keep in mind quality over quantity. You don't need much to make these toys, so it's worth using the best-quality materials for your special projects.

Yarn

Choosing a yarn for your project is part of the fun of personalizing your creation! It's always a good idea to keep the age of your recipient in mind when choosing what kind of yarn to use.

For very young children who like to put everything in their mouths, it might be prudent to go with organic or natural fibers, such as cotton or wool (but always be sure to check for allergies first). Blended yarns are wonderful, as they often combine the best qualities of their respective fibers. Acrylic yarns can also make excellent toys, as they are fairly easy to clean and care for and are generally less expensive than natural-fiber yarns.

The projects in this book call for worsted-weight yarn and a size G-6 (4 mm) hook, or DK-weight yarn and a size E-4 (3.5 mm) hook. You may find that the gauge of yarns can vary in thickness from one brand to another. Adjust your hook size accordingly so that your stitches stay close together. Because you're making stuffed animals and not garments, your stitch gauge and overall sizing is not crucial. Just be sure you're crocheting a firm fabric that won't allow stuffing to show through.

To adjust the size of a toy, choose a lighter- or heavier-weight yarn. For example, if you wish to make a family of cows, you could use a DK-weight yarn and a size D-3 (3.25 mm) or E-4 (3.5 mm) hook to make a calf, or go jumbo and make a big bull by using bulky-weight yarn and a size I-9 (5.5 mm) hook. Refer to the standard yarn-weight chart on page 76 for more information.

As a general rule, 125 to 150 yards of worsted-weight yarn should be more than enough to make one toy.

Stuffing

Most craft and fabric stores carry polyester fiberfill, although more locations now carry natural fiber and organic options as well. Fiberfill stuffing will maintain its loft over time and hold up well to the wear and tear of play and cleaning.

For natural fibers, the Internet can be a great resource for specialty stuffing, such as organic wool and organic cotton. Check out the resources page (page 78) for where you can find organic and natural stuffing.

Fiberfill, cotton, and wool stuffing (from left to right)

Crochet Hooks

Crochet hooks vary in size, color, and material. I prefer metal hooks, because they're strong and don't bend while crocheting. For the most accurate sizing, go by the millimeter sizing on the hook since different manufacturers use a range of markings and systems like numbers or letters. (See "Crochet Hook Sizes" on page 76.)

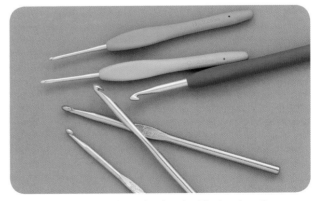

Assortment of crochet hooks. Notice that the ergonomic ones (top) have a wider grip than traditional crochet hooks (bottom), which may feel better in your hands.

Stitch Counters and Slip Rings

Most of these patterns are worked in a continuous spiral. A stitch or row counter, combined with the use of slip rings or safety pins marking the beginning of each round, can help you keep track of which round you are currently working on. You can also use slip rings to hold the edges of two crochet pieces together as you sew an edge closed.

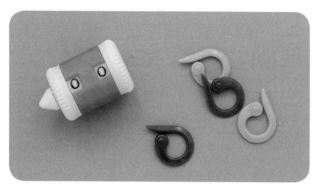

Mechanical row counters and slip-ring stitch markers make it easy to keep track of your work.

Sticky Notes and Pencils

I always keep a small stack of sticky notes and a mechanical pencil in my notions bag. That way, when I need to stop midway through a project, I can stick a note right on the page in my pattern book and jot down exactly where I left off in the pattern. I'll sometimes just draw an arrow on the sticky note and line up the arrow with my current row so I can easily find my place when I come back to my project.

Eyes

Knowing who the recipient of the toy will be will help you determine which eye option is most suitable.

Use the eye patterns on page 75 or make quick and easy black felt eyes by using various holes in a knitting needle gauge to trace the perfect size down to the millimeter. A white gel pen should produce a nice visible line while tracing. Felt eyes can be attached using a needle and thread, or with washable fabric glue.

Plastic eyes with safety backings are available at craft stores and on the Internet. My favorite online resource is Etsy shop 6060 (see "Resources" on page 78), where you can pick up a variety of hard-to-find sizes and colors. The plastic backings, once applied, are designed not to come off again, but it's

recommended you insert the eye post through the plies of a yarn strand before securing the backing to keep smaller-sized eyes (4 to 6 mm) from pushing back into the toy after being installed.

A variety of plastic safety eyes from Etsy shop 6060

For children under three, I strongly recommend French knots for eyes, as the plastic eyes can become a choking hazard if removed. See page 71 for instructions, and page 72 for a tip on how to bulk up your French knots.

Felt

Craft felt comes in a variety of colors and fiber contents, such as polyester, acrylic, wool, and bamboo. If using wool and bamboo felt, you can either hand wash your toys in cool water or prewash your felt before cutting out and attaching the pieces to your toy, making the final toy machine washable (on gentle cycle). You can choose thread that matches your felt, or you can go for a fun patchwork look and use a contrasting color.

A selection of wool and bamboo felt from American Felt and Craft, organic threads from NearSea Naturals, and traditional cotton threads from Gütermann

When tracing shapes onto felt, a ballpoint pen or blunted No. 2 pencil works fairly well on light colors, while a white gel pen works best on darker colors. Cut inside the lines so that the marks will not show.

Cutting Tools

Consider investing in a high-quality pair of scissors for cutting out felt shapes, and a smaller pair of embroidery scissors for trimming threads and loose ends. Use these scissors only on your crocheted projects to keep the blade nice and sharp.

Steel Tapestry Needles

A few steel tapestry needles will make assembling your farm animals a snap. Skip the plastic tapestry needles, since they can sometimes bend when going through thick materials like felt or a tightly stuffed toy. Sew finished toy parts and open edges together, and make French-knot eyes using a large tapestry needle (size 13) with worsted-weight yarn, or a smaller tapestry needle (size 17) with DK- or sport-weight yarn. For easier threading, look for needles with big eyes. A size 20 or 22 embroidery or chenille needle is good for sewing on eyes and embroidering other details.

Straight Pins

Straight pins (or marking pins) with round glass or plastic heads can be a huge help in holding all your toy's pieces together and patches in place before sewing everything down. I find that the ones with big round heads are the easiest to handle.

Noisemakers

To add a little more zing to your chicken or a ring to your cow, you can purchase a variety of noisemakers like bells, squeakers, crinkle paper, or rattles to insert into the body of your farm animal.

Noisemakers from American Felt and Craft

Crochet Stitches

This section will provide an overview of all the stitches used for the patterns in this book. Since most of the patterns use only a few basic stitches, they make great projects for beginners.

Slipknot

❶ Make a loop with your yarn, leaving a 6" tail.

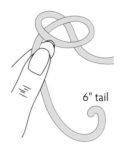

6" tail

❷ Insert the hook into the loop and gently pull up and tighten the yarn around the hook. The tail will be woven into your finished piece.

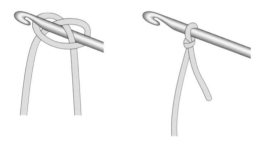

Yarn Over (YO)

Wrap the yarn over your hook from back to front.

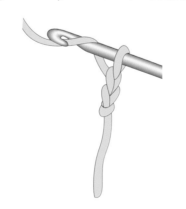

Chain (ch)

Make a slipknot and place it on your hook. You'll have one loop on your hook.

❶ Yarn over the hook with the working yarn.

❷ Catch the yarn with your hook and draw it through the loop on your hook. You will now have a new loop on your hook with the slipknot below it.

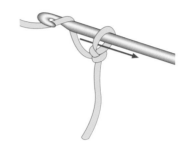

❸ Repeat steps 1 and 2 to make as many chains as indicated in the pattern. When checking your count, keep in mind that you should skip the loop currently on the hook and only count the chains below it.

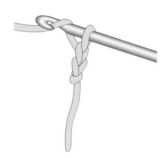

Slip Stitch (sl st)

Slip stitches can be used to move yarn across multiple stitches without adding additional height to the row. Start by inserting your hook into the next chain or stitch, yarn over the hook, and pull through both loops on the hook in one motion. You'll have one remaining loop on your hook.

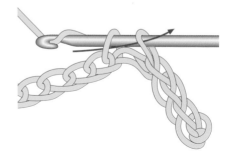

Single Crochet (sc)

❶ Insert your hook into the indicated chain or stitch in the pattern, yarn over the hook, and pull through the chain or stitch. You'll have two loops on your hook.

❷ Yarn over the hook and pull through both loops on your hook to complete the stitch. You'll have one loop on your hook.

Front-Post Single Crochet (FPsc)

❶ Insert your hook below the next stitch into the space on the right side of the stitch's post, bring your hook back out on the left side of the post, and yarn over the hook.

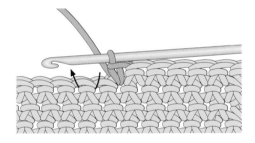

❷ Draw the yarn through and around the back of the post. You'll have two loops on the hook. Yarn over the hook and draw through both loops on the hook to finish the stitch.

Half Double Crochet (hdc)

❶ Yarn over the hook and insert the hook into the indicated chain or stitch in the pattern. Yarn over

the hook and pull through the chain or stitch. You'll have three loops on your hook.

❷ Yarn over the hook and pull through all three loops on the hook to complete the stitch. You'll have one loop on your hook.

Double Crochet (dc)

❶ Yarn over the hook and insert the hook into the indicated chain or stitch in the pattern.

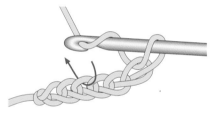

❷ Yarn over the hook and pull through the chain or stitch. You'll have three loops on your hook.

❸ Yarn over the hook and pull through two loops on the hook. You'll have two loops remaining on your hook.

④ Yarn over the hook and pull through the last two loops on the hook to complete the stitch. You'll have one loop on your hook.

Triple Crochet (tr)

❶ Yarn over the hook twice and insert the hook into the indicated chain or stitch in the pattern. Yarn over the hook and pull through the chain or stitch. You'll have four loops on your hook.

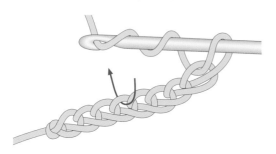

❷ Yarn over the hook and pull through two loops on the hook. You'll have three loops on your hook.

❸ Yarn over the hook and pull through two loops on the hook. You'll have two loops on your hook.

④ Yarn over the hook and pull through the last two loops on the hook to complete the stitch. You'll have one loop on your hook.

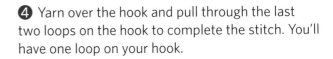

Single-Crochet Increase

You'll see most of the patterns in this book indicate "sc 2 in next st" when an increase is needed. To work an increase, simply work the number of stitches specified into the same stitch.

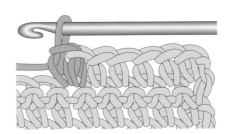

Single-Crochet Decrease (sc2tog)

All the patterns in this book use single-crochet decreases to reduce the number of stitches in a row or round.

❶ Insert your hook into the next stitch, yarn over the hook, and pull through the stitch, leaving a loop on your hook. You'll have two loops on your hook.

❷ Repeat step 1 in the next stitch. You'll have three loops on your hook.

❸ Yarn over the hook and pull through all three loops. You'll have one loop on your hook.

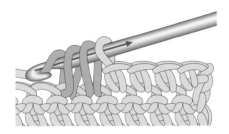

Invisible Single-Crochet Decrease (sc2tog)

This technique can be used instead of the standard single-crochet decrease. It helps eliminate the spaces that sometimes appear in the surface of your toy as you make your decreases.

❶ Insert your hook into the front loop of the next stitch and then immediately into the front loop of the following stitch. You will have three loops on your hook.

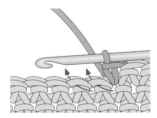

❷ Yarn over and draw the working yarn through the two front loops on the hook. You'll have two loops on your hook.

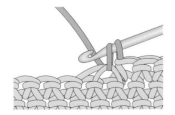

❸ Yarn over the hook and pull through both loops on your hook to complete the stitch. You'll have one loop on your hook.

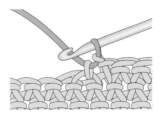

Working in a Spiral Round

The projects in this book are worked in a spiral round in which there are no slip stitches or chains between rounds. You just keep crocheting from one round to the next. It can be helpful to use stitch markers and row counters.

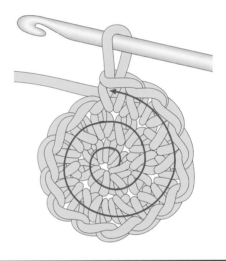

Using Stitch Markers

To keep track of the round you're currently working on, place a stitch marker in the last stitch of the round you just worked. You'll know you've come to the end of a round when you reach the stitch with the marker. After removing the marker, work the last stitch in the round, replace the marker in the new last stitch, and begin working the next round.

Adjustable Ring

The adjustable ring is a great technique that can take care of the unsightly hole in the middle of your starting round.

1 Form a ring with your yarn, leaving a 6" tail. Insert the hook into the loop as shown, as if you were making a slipknot.

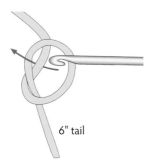

6" tail

2 Yarn over the hook and pull through the loop to make a slip stitch.

3 Chain one and then single crochet the number of stitches indicated in the pattern, taking care to enclose both strands of yarn that make up the adjustable ring. To close the center of the ring, pull tightly on the 6" yarn tail. Your adjustable ring is now complete.

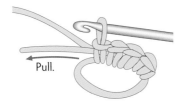

Pull.

To start the next round, work your next stitch in the first single crochet of the adjustable ring. If you need to make a semicircle shape (like for an ear), you'll be instructed to chain one and turn the work so that the wrong side of the work is facing

you. You can then crochet into the single-crochet stitches of the adjustable ring as indicated in the pattern.

Working around a Chain

A few patterns begin by working around a chain of stitches. After creating your chain, you'll first work in the back ridge loops of the chain and then in the front loops of the chain.

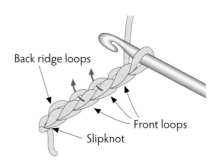

Back ridge loops

Front loops

Slipknot

1 Make a chain as per the pattern instructions.

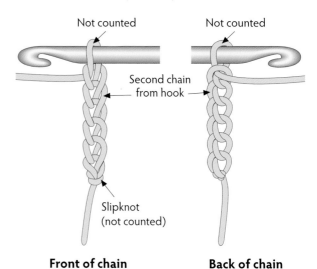

Not counted

Not counted

Second chain from hook

Slipknot (not counted)

Front of chain

Back of chain

2 For round 1, starting in the second chain from the hook, work your first stitch in the back ridge loop of the chain and mark it with a slip or locking ring. Continue working down the chain into the back ridge loops until you've reached the last chain next to the slipknot. Work the indicated number of stitches into the back ridge loop of this last chain.

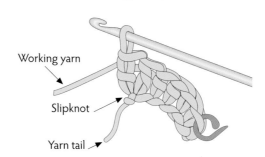

Working yarn

Slipknot

Yarn tail

❸ When you're ready to work the other side of the chain, rotate your work so the front loops of the chain are facing up. Starting in the next chain (i.e., the second chain from the slipknot), insert your hook into the space under the two front loops of the chain stitch to work your stitch.

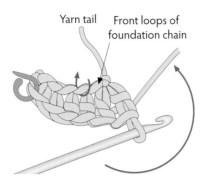

Yarn tail   Front loops of
foundation chain

Rotate and work in
front loops of chain.

❹ Continue in the pattern until you reach the end of round 1. For patterns that instruct you to continue on to round 2, begin your new round in the marked first stitch of round 1.

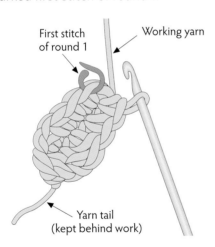

First stitch
of round 1   Working yarn

Yarn tail
(kept behind work)

Right Side (RS) versus Wrong Side (WS)

When working in the round, it's important to keep track of which side of your pattern is the right side, as it will affect which part of the stitch you'll perceive as the back loop versus the front loop. For pieces that begin with an adjustable ring, the 6" tail left over from forming the ring will usually lie on the wrong side of the piece.

Back Loops (bl) and Front Loops (fl)

Unless otherwise indicated, you'll be working in both loops of a stitch except when the pattern instructs that a stitch should be worked in the back loop or front loop only. When viewing your piece from the right side, the back loop will be the loop farthest away while the front loop is the loop closest to you.

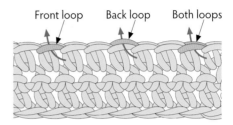

Front loop   Back loop   Both loops

Fastening Off

After you've completed your last stitch, cut the yarn, leaving at least a 6" tail. To fasten the yarn off, draw this tail through the last loop on your hook and pull firmly to secure it. In many cases, you can use the long tail to sew other pieces to the body or to sew up a seam.

Changing Colors

Changing colors requires a little reading ahead, since a new color is actually introduced while you are completing the last stitch of the old color. Work the stitch prior to the color change up to the last step in which you would normally pull the yarn through the loop(s) on your hook to complete the stitch. To change colors, YO the hook with your new color and draw the new color through the remaining loop(s) on your hook to complete the stitch. You can then continue on to the next stitch in the new color.

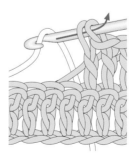

For color changes at the beginning of a new row, complete the stitch in your previous row, and then introduce the new color as you ch 1 and turn. Continue to work with your new color for the next row.

Crocheting on the Surface

Crocheting on the surface of your piece is a great way to add a fluffy, woolly coat to your creations. Patterns that call for this technique will use it in a very free-form kind of way so that the stitches are simply placed wherever you think they should go. For this example, we'll go over single crochet, but you can also make a line of slip stitches, half double crochet, or double crochet on the surface of your work as well using the same technique.

❶ On the right side of your work, insert your hook through the surface stitch of your piece, yarn over the hook, and draw a loop back out through the surface stitch. You'll have one loop on your hook.

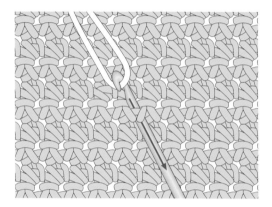

❷ Insert your hook into a space very close to your starting point and draw out another loop of yarn through the surface of your piece. You'll have two loops on your hook. Yarn over the hook in preparation for making the single crochet in the next step.

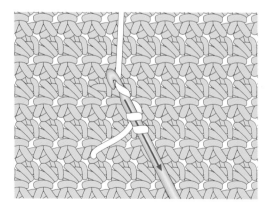

❸ Pull the yarn through the two loops. You've just made a single crochet on the surface of your piece.

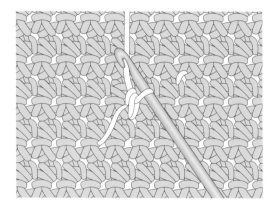

❹ Repeat steps 2 and 3 to create a free-form line of single crochet along the surface of your piece. Depending on the pattern instructions, you may continue to work additional rows into these stitches. Fasten off and weave in ends when finished.

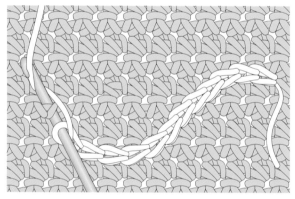

Simple embroidery stitches are useful for adding details like toes and eyebrows, for shaping the surface of your toy, and for attaching final details like felt pieces.

Running Stitch

The running stitch is primarily used to sew on felt patches but can also be used for curving and securing simple surface shaping. It can also be used to attach crochet pieces. Simply pass the needle and thread in and out of the fabric in a dashed-line pattern.

Long Stitch

A long stitch is great for shaping the surface of your toy. With your yarn and a metal tapestry needle, draw the yarn up through the surface of your piece and then reinsert the needle in a different location. Repeat if desired to double or triple the yarn. To cinch and shape the surface of your piece, pull the yarn firmly as you work.

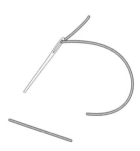

Satin Stitch

The satin stitch is used to create the beaks on the chickens. To work, start by drawing the yarn through the surface of your work from point A to point B and loop back around to reinsert the needle

next to point A. Work the number of satin stitches close together from point A to point B as directed in the pattern.

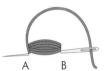

Lazy Daisy Stitch Variation

Use this variation of the lazy daisy stitch to create arched eyebrows. Draw the yarn up through the surface of your piece at point A where you want the eyebrow to begin. Reinsert the needle where you want the arch to end at point B, leaving the yarn loose enough to achieve a nice arch. To anchor the arched shape, draw the yarn up at the top of the arch at point C and reinsert it at point D, making a small stitch to hold the arch in place.

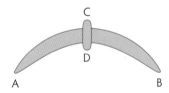

French Knot

French-knot eyes are ideal for baby-safe toys and can be used in place of plastic safety eyes. Bring the yarn up from the wrong side to the right side at the spot where you want the eye. With the yarn and needle on the right side of the work, hold the yarn close to the surface of the work where the yarn has most recently emerged and wind the yarn around the needle four or five times (depending on how big an eye you would like to make). While still applying tension to the yarn, insert the needle close to where the yarn initially came out and pull the needle through to the wrong side, leaving a knot on the surface.

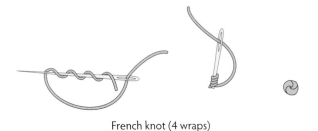

French knot (4 wraps)

To bulk up the French knot, draw the needle and yarn out at the base of the completed French knot and proceed to wind the yarn around the base of the French knot three or four times.

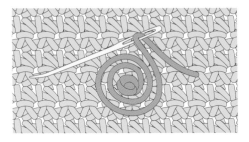

To secure, draw the needle through the top surface of the French knot to catch a few loops, and then pull tightly.

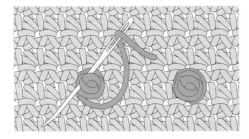

Finishing Touches

For the best results when putting your toy together, follow these helpful finishing tips and tricks.

Putting It All Together

To ensure your pattern pieces end up in the right spots, look over photos and illustrations for each toy before you begin assembly and use marking pins to help you work out the placement of the various pieces before sewing everything together. Slip-ring markers can also be very useful in holding a long seam together as you work.

For legs and arms, lay the closed seams flat against the body and whipstitch them in place with the leftover yarn tail. When attaching open edges of tails and muzzles or a head to a body, the mattress seam can provide a close, tight seam between pieces. If you find it tricky to keep your leg placement even, use a couple of large straight pins to pin the various pieces into position to make sure your placement will work, and your animal can stand, before you start sewing.

Whipstitch

To close an opening, pinch the open edges together with your fingers. Using your tapestry needle and leftover yarn tail, draw the needle and yarn through your piece, making sure to catch both edges. Pull the yarn up and over the edge of the work before pulling the needle through both edges again, in a spiral-like motion. Continue until the seam is closed.

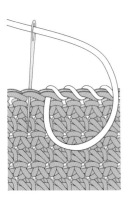

Mattress Seam

Choose a point on the surface or edge of your first piece and insert the needle from A to B under a single stitch and pull the yarn through. Cross over to the opposite surface and draw your needle under a single stitch from C to D with the entry point at C lining up between points A and B on the first surface. Return to the first surface and insert your needle directly next to (or above if you're working vertically) exit point B. Continue to work back and forth in this manner until the seam is closed, pulling firmly after every few stitches to ensure a clean, closed seam.

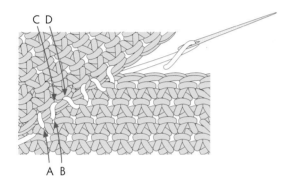

Closing Round Holes

For closing round holes like the ones on heads and body shapes, thread the remaining yarn tail onto a tapestry needle. Following the edge of the opening, insert the needle through just the front loop of each single crochet, effectively winding the tail around the front loop of the stitches. When you've worked all the way around the opening, pull the tail firmly to close the hole (just like you were cinching a drawstring bag closed).

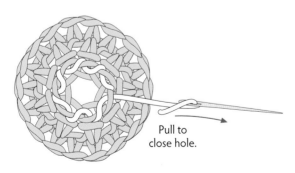

Pull to close hole.

Fringe Technique

Use this technique to apply manes, tails, and hair to your toys. You'll need your crochet hook and enough pieces of yarn to cover the desired area. It's always better to cut the pieces a little longer and trim them down after they've been applied. To make quick work of cutting the yarn for manes, tails, and hair, try winding the yarn around three or four fingers (depending on how long you want the pieces to be), and then cut all the loops at once.

❶ To apply fringe, choose a spot on the toy to add a strand of yarn and insert your crochet hook under that surface stitch. Fold the strand of yarn over your crochet hook and draw it back through the surface of the toy, forming a small loop.

❷ Pull the loose ends of the yarn through the loop and pull tightly to knot it.

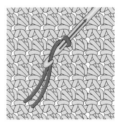

❸ Use a steel tapestry needle to separate the yarn strands for a fuller look before trimming to the desired length.

Yarn Ends

It can become pesky business having to deal with attaching, tying off, and weaving in yarn ends when making embroidery stitches. To make things a bit easier, try this trick. Starting with a new piece of yarn, insert your needle about an inch from where you intend to start your embroidery and leave a 4" tail. Bring the needle up at the first stitch. Hold the yarn tail down with your fingers as you work the first couple of stitches until the yarn appears to feel secure. When you finish your last stitch, bring the needle out at the same spot of the beginning tail and cut the end, leaving another 4" tail. Knot the two yarn tails together, and then use a crochet hook or tapestry needle to draw the yarn and the knot back through the hole. It might take a bit of a tug to pull the knot and yarn tails through, but everything will be nice and hidden.

Attaching Felt Patches

Pin felt patches in place before you start sewing them to your toy. My preferred stitch for attaching felt is the running stitch (page 71), but a whipstitch (page 72) can work well too.

If you prefer to glue your patches to your work instead of sewing with a needle and thread, consider picking up washable fabric glue (look for Fabri-Tac or Aleene's brands of washable fabric glue).

Double Threading a Needle

Do this for a little extra thread strength when sewing felt shapes onto your toys. Cut a piece of thread twice as long as you normally would need for sewing around the shape. Fold the thread in half and insert the cut ends into the eye of the sewing needle to create a big loop. Pass the needle in and out of the surface of your toy, pulling the thread partially through until the loop is only 2" or 3" long at the surface of your work. Guide your needle through this small loop and pull gently to tighten the loop. Once your thread is secured, you can then sew on your felt patch with the doubled thread.

Caring for Your Toys

The following guidelines will help you care for your toys. First and foremost, please refer to the labels from your selected yarns for guidance on the most appropriate cleaning methods for your particular projects. If you are giving your toy as a gift, consider including a yarn label in the gift package for the recipient. You want to be as gentle as possible when cleaning your toys to ensure that the shaping and details are preserved.

If the yarn label allows it, I recommend hand washing for most toys (especially if the toy has plastic eyes or felt details) in cool or lukewarm water. Detergents and gentle soaps like Soak or Woolite will do a good job cleaning your crocheted toy. After washing your toy in soapy water, you'll need to rinse the soap out before rolling the toy up in a towel to help gently wring out the extra water. Allow the toy to air dry in a well-ventilated area.

For toys that don't have felt patches or plastic eyes, you could give the washer and dryer a go if the care instructions for the yarn you've used allow it. Place the toy in a lingerie bag, clean it on a gentle cycle in your washer, and then dry it in the dryer on low heat or let it air dry.

Patterns

You can make templates for felt patches using tracing paper or a photocopier/scanner, or by downloading and printing the patterns from ShopMartingale.com/extras or MKCrochet.com/resources. For attaching felt patches, refer to page 74.

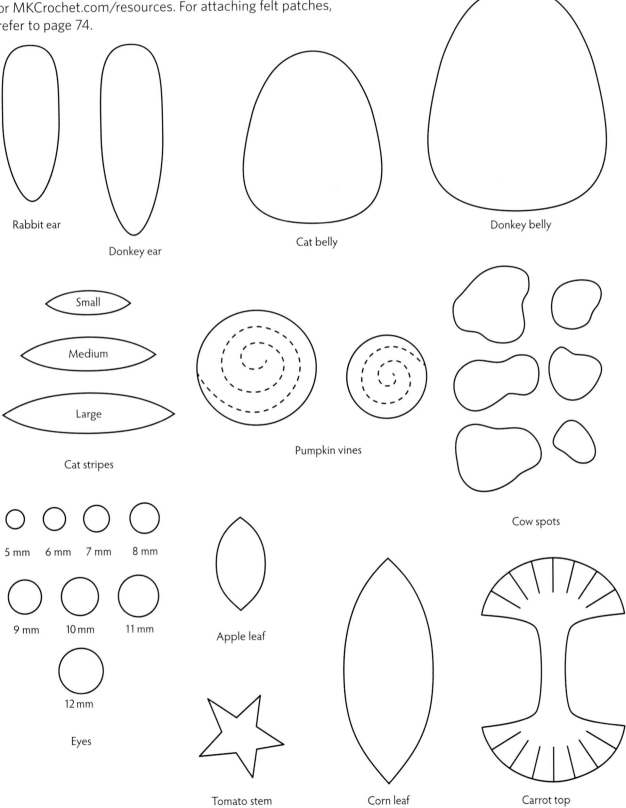

Rabbit ear

Donkey ear

Cat belly

Donkey belly

Small

Medium

Large

Cat stripes

Pumpkin vines

Cow spots

5 mm   6 mm   7 mm   8 mm

9 mm   10 mm   11 mm

12 mm

Eyes

Apple leaf

Tomato stem

Corn leaf

Carrot top

Abbreviations

*	repeat instructions following the single asterisk as directed
approx	approximately
beg	begin(ning)
bl	back loop(s)
CC	contrasting color
ch(s)	chain(s) or chain stitch(es)
cont	continue(ing)(s)
dc	double crochet(s)
dec(s)	decrease(ing)(s)
fl	front loop(s)
FPsc	front post single crochet
hdc	half double crochet(s)
inc(s)	increase(ing)(s)
lp(s)	loop(s)
MC	main color
mm	millimeter(s)
rep(s)	repeat(s)
rnd(s)	round(s)
RS	right side
sc	single crochet(s)
sc2tog	single crochet 2 stitches together—1 stitch decreased
sk	skip
sl st(s)	slip stitch(es)
sp(s)	space(s)
st(s)	stitch(es)
tog	together
tr	triple crochet
WS	wrong side
yd(s)	yard(s)
YO	yarn over

Standard Yarn Weights

Yarn-Weight Symbol and Category Name	1 Super Fine	2 Fine	3 Light	4 Medium	5 Bulky	6 Super Bulky
Types of Yarn in Category	Sock, Fingering, Baby	Sport, Baby	DK, Light Worsted	Worsted, Afghan, Aran	Chunky, Craft, Rug	Bulky, Roving
Crochet Gauge* Range in Single Crochet to 4"	21 to 32 sts	16 to 20 sts	12 to 17 sts	11 to 14 sts	8 to 11 sts	5 to 9 sts
Recommended Hook in Metric Size Range	2.25 to 3.5 mm	3.5 to 4.5 mm	4.5 to 5.5 mm	5.5 to 6.5 mm	6.5 to 9 mm	9 mm and larger
Recommended Hook in U.S. Size Range	B-1 to E-4	E-4 to 7	7 to I-9	I-9 to K-10½	K-10½ to M-13	M-13 and larger

*These are guidelines only. The above reflect the most commonly used gauges and hook sizes for specific yarn categories.

Skill Levels

■□□□ **Beginner:** Projects for first-time crocheters using basic stitches; minimal shaping.

■■□□ **Easy:** Projects using yarn with basic stitches, repetitive stitch patterns, simple color changes, and simple shaping and finishing.

■■■□ **Intermediate:** Projects using a variety of techniques, such as basic lace patterns or color patterns; midlevel shaping and finishing.

■■■■ **Experienced:** Projects with intricate stitch patterns, techniques, and dimension, such as nonrepeating patterns, multicolor techniques, fine threads, small hooks, detailed shaping, and refined finishing.

Crochet Hook Sizes

Millimeter	US Size*
2.25 mm	B-1
2.75 mm	C-2
3.25 mm	D-3
3.5 mm	E-4
3.75 mm	F-5
4 mm	G-6
4.5 mm	7
5 mm	H-8
5.5 mm	I-9
6 mm	J-10
6.5 mm	K-10½
8 mm	L-11
9 mm	M/N-13

*Letter or number may vary. Rely on the millimeter sizing.

Yarns Used

Hen and Rooster
Lion Brand Superwash Merino in Ivory, Mahogany, Cayenne, Dijon, Night Sky, and Sky

Chick
Lion Brand Baby Soft Yarn in Pastel Yellow
Lion Brand Superwash Merino in Dijon

Duck
Lion Brand Superwash Merino in Ivory, Night Sky, and Dijon

Duckling
Lion Brand Baby Soft Yarn in White
Lion Brand Superwash Merino in Dijon

Rabbit
Lion Brand Angora Merino in Vanilla and Parchment
Lion Brand Superwash Merino in Night Sky

Pig
Knit Picks Swish Worsted Yarn in Carnation and Black

Piglets
Knit Picks Swish DK Yarn in Carnation and Coal

Holstein Cow
Red Heart Soft in Black, Rose Blush, Honey, and Off White

Brown Jersey Cow
Red Heart Soft in Chocolate, Toast, Off White, Black, and Charcoal

Black Angus Bull
Red Heart Soft in Black, Wheat, Off White, and Charcoal

Holstein Calf
Red Heart Anne Geddes Baby in Night-Night, Lily, Daffodil, and Rosie

Horse
Red Heart Soft in Chocolate, Toast, Black, and Charcoal

Foal
Red Heart Anne Geddes Baby in Teddy, Dolphin, and Night-Night

Donkey
Red Heart Soft in Light Grey Heather, Off White, and Black

Sheep and Lambs
Red Heart Soft in Charcoal, Black, and Off White
Red Heart Light and Lofty in Cafe Au Lait, Onyx, and Puff

Alpaca
Berroco Ultra Alpaca in Couscous, Brown Rice, and Mahogany Mix
Knit Picks Swish Worsted Yarn in Black

Baby Alpaca
Lion Brand Baby Alpaca Yarn in Natural, Tan, and Auburn
Lion Brand Superwash Merino in Night Sky

Goat and Kid
Red Heart Soft in White, Black, Honey, and Charcoal

Sheepdog
Knit Picks Swish DK Yarn in Coal, White, and Marble Heather

Cat
Knit Picks Swish DK Yarn in Allspice, White, Coal, and Carnation

Mouse
Knit Picks Swish DK Yarn in Dove Heather, Coal, and Carnation

Hay Bundle
Knit Picks Swish Worsted Yarn in Honey
Knit Picks Swish DK Yarn in Bark

Milk Pail
Knit Picks Swish DK Yarn in White, Marble Heather, and Bark

Pumpkin
Knit Picks Swish DK Yarn in Allspice and Bark

Apple
Knit Picks Swish DK Yarn in Green Tea Heather and Serrano

Tomato
Knit Picks Swish DK Yarn in Garnet Heather

Carrot
Knit Picks Swish DK Yarn in Orange

Corn
Knit Picks Swish DK Yarn in Cornmeal and Honey

Egg
Knit Picks Swish DK Yarn in White, Doe, and Camel Heather

Resources

If you're interested in trying some of the yarns or tools used in this book, please check out the following resources!

6060
www.6060.etsy.com
Online retailer of a variety of unique plastic safety eyes

American Felt and Craft
www.americanfeltandcraft.com
Online retailer of wool felt and toy noisemaker inserts

Berroco
www.berroco.com
Fine hand-knitting yarns, available at yarn shops

Clover
www.clover-usa.com
Hooks and notions, available at local craft stores

Coats and Clark
www.coatsandclark.com
Red Heart yarn, available at local craft stores

Fiskars
www.fiskars.com
Scissors and cutting mats, available at local craft stores

Hobbs Bonded Fibers
www.hobbsbondedfibers.com
Poly-down fiberfill toy stuffing and black batting, available at local craft stores

Knit Picks
www.knitpicks.com
Fine yarns and notions, available online

Lion Brand
www.lionbrandyarn.com
Lion Brand yarn, available at local craft stores

NearSea Naturals
www.nearseanaturals.com
Online retailer of sustainable, natural, and organic stuffing and thread

Acknowledgments

It is with much gratitude and appreciation for the support of my friends, family, and the publishing team at Martingale that my third book was made possible!

Thanks to:

My husband, Michael, who encourages me to make time in my life to design and create (even if it means making our house into a yarn-festooned mess in the process).

My parents, who nurtured my love of art since I could hold a pencil (or a crochet hook).

Ursula Reikes and Tiffany Mottet for taking such amazing care in checking and editing all the patterns.

Paula Schlosser, Brent Kane, and Connor Chin for creating such a beautiful book.

Karen Burns, Karen Soltys, and Jennifer Keltner for allowing me to round out my series of crocheted-creation patterns with a third book.

And, finally, to my children, James and Emily, who inspire me to be creative every day.

To make one or more farmers to tend your crocheted farm, download the free pattern at ShopMartingale.com/extras.

Megan Kreiner grew up on Long Island, New York, in a household where art and art projects were a daily part of life. Coming from a long line of knitters and crocheters, Megan learned the craft at an early age from her grandmother, her aunt, and her mother. Since 2012, her MK Crochet and MK Knits pattern lines have been published and featured in books and various crochet and knitting magazines.

A graduate with a fine arts degree in computer graphics and animation from the University of Massachusetts, Amherst, Megan is pursuing a career in the feature animation industry in Los Angeles. She is an animator at DreamWorks Animation.

Megan lives in Altadena, California, with her husband, Michael, and their children, James and Emily. View her work at MKCrochet.com.

mk crochet ®